Photography by Marianne Majerus

rob cassy

101 IDEAS
gardens

quadrille

For Martin Breese

Editorial Director Jane O'Shea
Art Director Helen Lewis
Designer Paul Welti
Project Editor Hilary Mandleberg
Production Rebecca Short
Photography Marianne Majerus

First published in 2005 by
Quadrille Publishing Limited
Alhambra House
27–31 Charing Cross Road
London WC2H oLS

British Library Cataloguing-in-Publication
Data. A catalogue record for this book is
available from the British Library.

ISBN 1-84400-130-X

Every effort has been made to ensure the
accuracy of the information in this book.
In no circumstances can the publisher or
the author accept any liability for any
loss, injury or damage of any kind
resulting from any error in or omission
from the information contained in this
book..

Printed in China

contents

part two
getting down to the detail

part three
keeping it fresh

part one

the big picture

1 candid camera

Take a long cool look at your outdoor space. Not just from one vantage point but from as many as possible.

take a look

Be honest about what you see. Note features that you like as well as areas with room for improvement. Well-focussed mental snapshots are powerful design tools. The more intimately you're acquainted with any garden, the better equipped you are to improve it.

don't just stand and stare

Pace around your plot. A garden is a place for people, so it's important to get a feel for the space with your body. Understand its proportions in relation to your height and to the stride of your feet. Don't worry about measuring up just yet.

gut reaction

Do you feel exhilarated on entering your garden, or does it make you feel depressed? Gardening isn't just about the mind and body, it's about the spirit too. Analyse your feelings if you can. What might change them for the better?

all change

Visit your garden at different times of the day to observe how the quality of light changes as the sun moves through the sky. Take especial note of areas that are always warm and bright, and watch out for places in perpetual gloom.

evening event

Wander outside as evening falls. Particularly in a city, the garden can be a thrilling place at night time, somewhere perfect for summer entertaining. If you were to install lighting, what kind of atmosphere would you like to create?

good neighbours

Peep through the hedge, peek through gaps in the fence or even peer over the garden wall. Rubberneck your neighbours' balconies. Stare out across the rooftops. Best of all, invite yourself around. Be inspired by other people's efforts – and learn from their mistakes.

family and friends

Seek the advice of family and friends. Ask for their first impressions. A fresh pair of eyes can open up whole new horizons and frank opinions give great food for thought. Remember though: it's your garden, so it's your taste that counts.

legal eagle

Are there any legal restraints on what you can do outdoors? Local planning regulations, freeholds, leaseholds and deeds of covenant can hold strange surprises. Always check out your rights and obligations.

practicalities

Are there any practical limitations? Inspection covers for drains, pipes and cables should always be accessible; damp-proof courses should never be breached; rooftops, walls and balconies must be capable of bearing any load you place on them. Seek professional advice where necessary.

breathe in . . .

Now take a deep breath. You are about to become your very own garden designer. And relax. It's easier than you think!

2 over-exposed

North-facing or south-facing? Open to the east or to the west? People worry far too much about the aspect of their garden and its orientation to their home. So long as your garden faces up there's nothing to worry about. The sheer pointlessness of it all becomes apparent when you consider that a small rooftop garden and a large country estate face every which way. A town-house courtyard and a balcony in a city might have sunny aspects in theory, but that counts for nothing in practice when tall houses loom in at all sides or when there's a walloping great office block straight across the road.

And then there's global warming to consider, too. Perhaps it won't be long before moderately dry gardens turn into desert – or xeriscape – gardens, while low-lying gardens end up as a water wonderland.

Commonsense tells you soon enough whether you're sheltered from the wind or exposed to every gust and gale, and whether you're favoured by the sun or enveloped in shade, but sometimes a single garden will offer a surprising range of conditions. Whatever your situation, it's good to know what kind of plants thrive where so you can zoom in on them at garden centres and nurseries.

features of plants for over-exposed sites

- shiny, blue-grey or hard metallic leaves: these help deflect and reflect the sun's scorching rays.
- thorns: some drought-adapted plants, like the breathtaking sea holly *Eryngium giganteum*, protect their water reserves from grazing animals with prickly leaves.
- coatings: some develop cobweb or mealy coatings to hug back moisture that has been lost by surface evaporation.
- aromatic oils: some exude aromatic oils to seal themselves in a sticky gummy haze.
- wiry leaves and stems: fine-bladed grasses bow down before the wind then spring right back for more.

under-exposed

3

Chlorophyll is the green pigment that helps plants convert sunshine and fresh air into the energy they need for growth and dark-adapted plants positively glow with it. Some leaves grow large and umbrella-like to soak up every last ray. Others are closely arrayed in rows on gracefully arching stems. Ground-hugging plants generally have tiny leaves but the stems root as they go to weave dense, moss-like carpets. Moss itself can form soft emerald hummocks encrusting walls, pots and statues to glorious effect.

While many shade-loving plants have small insignificant flowers, others have real magic – seek out the extravagant tassels of *Garrya elliptica* in winter and the rose-petal blooms of *Helleborus niger*. If you have a craving for colour then spring bulbs can be permanent fixtures, but in summer and autumn it's wiser to punctuate the scene with seasonally themed containers using bought-in annuals already in bloom.

Replicate nature when planting in shadow, and aim for tiers of interest as though working up to the tree canopy from the forest floor. When you find that a species really thrives, try different varieties – bamboos, ferns and ivies in particular offer endless possibilities of size, shape and form.

A shady spot can be lush, opulent and tropical-looking. It can also be incredibly low-maintenance. Ordinary weeds won't flourish. Most plants will be evergreen, so they won't need an autumn tidy. Many will be slow-growing, so pruning and training can be done in a leisurely fashion.

features of plants for under-exposed sites

- evergreens
- rich green leaves
- cream or yellow variegation
- soft silvery leaves
- large, umbrella-like leaves
- closely arranged leaves on arching stems
- small insignificant flowers
- ground-hugging plants

romeo, romeo 4

Balconies have a ready-made charm and mystique. Associated in the popular imagination with historic buildings in capital cities, with seafront hotels and Mediterranean hideaways, they are easy assets to capitalise on.

Historically they were either purely decorative – a means of punctuating a façade with elaborate architectural detail – or strictly functional – for drying washing or airing bedding. Today they are about leisure and lifestyle.

The long, narrow space offered by a balcony is limited so be careful not to clutter it. Decorate it with just a few choice plants and pieces of furniture. You see everything up close, so quality counts. But you don't need much, so you won't break the bank.

Aim for a unified look. Metal containers and folding chairs are lightweight, smart, and look great together. Themed plantings look better than random arrangements. As ever, discipline and forethought pay the richest dividends.

the problem of privacy

Privacy is a curious issue here. You can watch the world around with impunity, and if you're overlooked by other buildings, who cares? But what is the etiquette with immediate neighbours? It's a bore to greet them every five minutes, and it's rude to blank them, but it's downright ridiculous to take turns outside. Nip any embarrassment in the bud with a well-chosen tree or shrub. Bays, box, black pines, citrus, cordylines and olives will all thrive. A head-height specimen means your eyes can't meet, and the problem vanishes! Trees grown as standards (lollipops) look especially smart and do the job with discretion.

key pointers for balconies
- avoid clutter
- use top-quality plants and materials
- match materials
- choose a theme
- head-height shrubs for privacy

on the roof 5

A roof garden is a privileged place. It offers panoramic views. It is hidden from the street. It is a floating island that allows free rein for your imagination. There is clean air to breathe and a blank canvas on which to paint a very personal picture.

A flat roof is entirely different to a roof garden and it is dangerous to confuse the two. Place a few pots and some furniture on a flat roof, subject it to heavy footfall and you'll soon jeopardise the ceiling below.

Now. Can a flat roof become a roof garden? Absolutely. Speak to a structural engineer, speak to your solicitor, speak to your local planning authority. The work won't come cheap but it will give you great pleasure and add value to your home.

five top tips

1 • Before buying anything large like a bench or a table, check that it will go in the lift or up the stairs. Self-assembly furniture is often the solution.

2 • If you suffer from air turbulence

on your roof garden, then anchor loungers, deckchairs and parasols to the floor. Should they sail off into the wild blue yonder they'll land you in court.

3 • Connect your pots to a watering system that will constantly replenish moisture lost to wind and sunshine. With the best will in the world, a watering can is rarely adequate in a hot summer: despite a thorough drenching before you leave for work, some plants can be gagging for another drink by lunchtime.

4 • Leaves and blooms are far less likely to get wind-scorched if you arrange containers in groups instead of rows – potted plants in clusters benefit from each other's protection.

5 • Don't worry if horticulture isn't high on your agenda. You can successfully create a beautiful garden with hard-landscaping materials alone.

6 within these walls

A courtyard garden is like a room without a ceiling: roll out the flooring, decorate the walls, then furnish it just so.

The more plants, decorative elements and furnishings that go into a courtyard garden, the less space there is for people. The more space you leave for people, the less stimulating their environment. Your challenge is to find the happy medium.

wall-to-wall comfort

• Use decorative flooring (see 38 and 39).
• Put the planting emphasis on the perimeter with flowering climbers and wall shrubs (see 50 and 51).
• Create seasonal interest with changing container displays of bought-in bedding. Hanging baskets, window boxes and flower swags provide great opportunities for planting without impinging one jot on the ground (see 75 and 76).
• Choose traditional folding or stacking garden furniture or invest in contemporary pieces suitable for indoor/outdoor use (see 16 and 55).
• Create the illusion of extra space with mirrors and trompe l'œil (see 46 and 48).

7 everything counts

Even the smallest and most unlikely bit of outdoors can be made more attractive. Skill and experience aren't half so important as a fertile imagination. Why put opaque glass in a downstairs loo when a generously planted window box can be admired from both sides and will be quite as convenient? Transform a side passage from a seedy thoroughfare into a burgeoning secret garden with a colourful lick of paint and a few well-chosen shade-lovers.

Work hard now on developing a tiny little space and just think of the returns you'll reap in future from larger and larger gardens attached to bigger and better homes.

needs

So tell me what you want, what you really really want!

somewhere to dry the washing?

Get a spring-loaded line like a giant tape measure that is quick and easy to string up and take down. If you want a permanent line, dark green nylon gives the best camouflage. Rotary driers are ugly as sin.

a shed for storage?

So you can hoard all your old rubbish? Why waste space that could accommodate a bench and some theatrically lit pots, a dining table and chairs, a playhouse, a water feature or a bed of fabulous plants?

a bin area?

Elaborate disguises simply attract attention. Paint bins to match the woodwork of your home, tuck them as far out of sight as possible, then simply forget about them.

security?

The garden is a buffer between your home and the world at large. Boundaries such as walls, fences and trellising reinforce it physically. Lighting, planting and a well-kept look reinforce it psychologically.

safety?

Take a balanced view of risks. Adults can be expected to watch out for spikes and thorns, to be wary of deep water, to know that some plants are poisonous and that others can irritate sensitive skin. Children can't, neither can pets. The elderly or disabled can have serious problems dealing with sudden changes in level. Never become paranoid, but always show consideration to others.

aspirations 9

make five wishes . . .

I'd like my garden to reflect my personality, my tastes and my travels.

I want it to be a place where I can always welcome family and friends.

I want almost all my time outdoors to be leisure and not hard labour.

To be honest, I'd like other people to be impressed by my achievements.

I'd also like to add value to my property and to increase its saleability.

. . . and do your best to grant them all

10 indulge your senses

We are all sensual creatures. Good gardens set every nerve in our body alight – truly great ones touch the soul.

sight

Sight more frequently, more extensively, and more importantly than any other sense gives us a direct relationship with the garden.

We see the garden from the home, so strive for attractive views from as many rooms as possible. Think of every pane of glass, each external doorway, as a picture frame around a painting.

Once actually in the garden, we experience visual stimuli all around, the eye drawing us towards anything of especial interest. Tempt viewers from one area to the next by laying a well-thought-out trail. Meandering pathways encourage us to move around a large garden, but the trick in a small one is to make the eye take a journey by itself. As lures, use decorative flooring, attractive boundaries, interesting furniture and flowerpots, plants that are colourful and curiously shaped.

A good garden will reveal more and more of itself (and more and more about its maker) the longer and harder you look. Build up relationships between objects to forge links involving colour, size and shape. Be a tease, too: anything that is partially obscured becomes, paradoxically, more rather than less interesting. What is that . . .?

Delight but don't confuse. Provide a restful focal point for the eye to alight on between its travels. Gazing long and idly upon one beautiful object is truly soothing.

smell

Close your eyes and breathe in slowly through your nose. Now imagine if every plant in every garden were chosen as much for its smell as for its looks. Pay more attention to scented flowers and aromatic foliage, and your garden will acquire a whole new dimension. Close to windows, beside walkways and alongside boundaries, exotic and unexpected fragrances will surprise and delight passers-by. Remember, too, that heavily scented blooms attract beautiful butterflies. Learn to savour the tang of dry earth after sudden rainfall, of freshly mown grass, of autumn leaves. Burn incense or scented candles in the still evening air.

hearing

Running, trickling and bubbling water; wind rustling through leaves or tinkling wind chimes; singing and chirruping birds; thrumming and buzzing insects – these aren't just incidental pleasures, they're essential, life-affirming forces to be embraced and incorporated into every garden. Adjust the flow of a pump to produce a pleasing sound. Grow bamboos and tall grasses and hear the breeze rustle through them. Put out food for the birds and hang up a few nesting boxes in spring – and be wary of pesticides.

A silent garden is a sad and sterile place.

touch

Touch is intimate and pleasurable. Just think of a hug, a kiss, a caress. Soft furry plants like lambs' ears (*Stachys byzantina*), silver sage (*Salvia argentea*), and mullein (*Verbascum bombyciferum*) positively beg us to stroke them. Few people can resist picking at the papery, peeling bark of trees like silver birch (*Betula papyrifera*), ornamental cherry (*Prunus serrula*) or the paper-bark maple (*Acer griseum*). We all tend to pat topiary balls on the head, and who doesn't feel like some great explorer when brushing aside the wayward branch of a shrub or the dangling stem of a climber? Build in a little temptation wherever you can. Go on, you know you want to.

taste

A full-blown kitchen garden is a taste explosion. Few of us have the time, space or energy to grow anything like all our own fruit and vegetables, but that doesn't mean we can't enjoy the flavours of fresh home-grown produce every now and again. Herbs can be grown virtually anywhere; apple trees, figs and grapevines can be trained against walls and fences; salad leaves can be smuggled into beds or cropped young in pots; the edible flower petals of nasturtiums, borage, mimosa and pot marigolds add an interesting bite to cold dishes.

the sixth sense

A garden that awakens all the senses will really bring you alive. And that will help make you, and all your visitors, happy and content.

There are so many schools and styles of garden design, so many critical approaches, that the human response is sometimes overlooked or forgotten. The bottom line is this: when something feels right, it is right.

budget 11

Money doesn't grow on trees . . .

hard landscaping –
five money-saving tips

1 • Far-fetched and dear-bought aren't always best. Imaginative combinations of everyday materials show that you've got style.

2 • Shop around. Builders' merchants are cheaper than garden centres. Salvage yards can be a steal.

3 • Remember to ask for a cash discount, a trade discount or a bulk discount. The answer is often 'yes'.

4 • Phase the work. There's no need to do everything at once. Whenever there's a little spare cash knocking around, invest it in the garden.

5 • If you're really pushing the boat out, consider financing your garden by increasing your mortgage.

soft landscaping – five money-saving tips

1 • Cultivate your friends and neighbours. People with well-established gardens always have plants to spare – make sure that some of them come your way.

2 • Learn how to propagate plants yourself by taking cuttings and by dividing large clumps of perennials. Use these as swaps.

3 • Nurseries in the countryside offer incredible value compared to retailers in cities. Track one down each time you're out of town.

4 • Patience is a virtue. Don't be tempted to buy large expensive plants. Smaller, cheaper specimens soon catch up once they're in the ground.

5 • Sow your own seeds. From little acorns, mighty oaks do grow.

a moving tale 12

A growing family, a job that requires frequent relocation, an ever-healthier bank balance. These are just a few of the reasons why we move house. Don't wait until you finally 'settle down' before becoming a gardener. Just imagine how many years of pleasure you'd lose.

Instead, start now. Even if you're not planning on staying anywhere long enough to put down serious roots, you can still have a beautiful garden. In fact, you deserve one. All you have to do is decorate your garden like an outdoor room and when it's time to move on all the best things can go with you in the back of the van – together with the contents of your home.

the garden you can take with you

- really great furniture
- luxuriant potted plants
- a freestanding water feature
- a big, bold sunshade
- a stylish barbecue

13 adapt and survive

Should a change in circumstances suggest a different gardening direction, go with the flow. If neighbours chop down a tree and flood your once shady garden with light, then it's time to adapt your planting. If a new block of flats suddenly overlooks you, create a little privacy for yourself. If you're starting a family, work towards a safe environment with built-in play value.

five easy adaptations

1 • Sick of mowing the lawn? Lift the turf and lay gravel.

2 • In need of privacy or shade? Build an arbour.

3 • Worried about children's safety? Slash your pond liner then fill it with play sand; dig up all your spiky plants and give them away.

4 • Concerned about a hard fall on concrete? Lay decking.

5 • At work all day? Install lighting and relax in your garden by night.

14 action plan

ready

Make a simple sketch of your outdoor space. Don't worry too much about drawing it to scale, just do the best you can. Then measure up and mark down all the dimensions. If your proportions were a bit wonky, it's now an easy matter to redraw the plan. Keep this with you at all times to check whether plants, ornaments and furniture will fit and to request approximate costings for landscaping materials.

steady

Turn everything over slowly in your mind's eye before making any commitments, and be sure to complete one task before moving on to the next. You don't have to revolutionise your garden at a single stroke; in fact little and often works best on both the practical and the financial level. Time is precious and you've got family and friends to attend to as well, so start small and learn as you go. Be realistic about what you can achieve by yourself and call in specialist help from carpenters, builders and electricians where necessary. And when there's heavy lifting to be done, get a helping hand from all those friends you've been cultivating.

go!

1 designer secrets

Successful design is less about imposing your will than letting the space achieve its unique potential. Here's how.

inside out

Humans are territorially minded, so gardens are generally designed from the boundary in. This keeps ravening wolves at bay and barricades your land against marauding tribes. In the modern world, better aesthetics are achieved by working from the inside out.

'x' marks the spot

Decide where you want to spend most of your time outdoors and what you want to do there. Then furnish that area accordingly. The optimum site will be sunny, accessible from the home, will afford ready access to the rest of your garden and will give great views of your surroundings. If you've been pacing your plot (see 1), a mental 'x' no doubt marks the spot already.

5 ideas

a sideways look

You'll need room to stretch your legs, and you'll want areas for planting. Paving, decking and lawns are often best oriented at oblique angles to your boundaries. This automatically creates deep and interestingly shaped flower pockets, and it takes attention away from the walls, fences, hedges or railings that hem you in. It is a deceptively simple idea that gives structure and form to plots with irregular shapes and that breaks down the stale uniformity of rectangular yards.

reach for the sky

A garden that concentrates on the ground plan is only ever two-dimensional. Add vertical accents to take possession of your airspace. Upright plants in pots, narrow trees and architectural supports for climbers encourage everyone to walk tall and proud.

open to suggestion

The ideal spaces for pots, ornaments and water features should now suggest themselves. Eyes are inevitably drawn into focus wherever two lines meet. Triangular groupings nicely fill out dead-ends, while circular bowls or arrangements ease the flow round sharp angles. No useable area need be lost. Simple

inside 16 outside

Where basement areas, patios and balconies adjoin a room it may be possible to effect an almost seamless transition using sliding doors, foldaway doors or French windows. The greater the transparency and access between the two, the better the effect.

If the combined space is to be used and read as one, the garden should contain elements of the home and the home should contain elements of the garden. Use the same kind of flowerpots indoors and out. Echo the style of planting and even some of the plants if you can.

So much wooden, plastic and metal furniture today is designed for home and garden alike that you can always find pieces for indoor and out to reflect one another and act as visual keys.

plants with passports

Many bamboos, citrus plants and palms are as happy indoors as out, as is the mock castor-oil plant, *Fatsia japonica*. Similarly, pots of spring-flowering bulbs indoors can echo those outside.

floors that flow

Polished stone floors indoors and out provide a continuous visual link whatever the weather. Stones with a rougher finish look softer but are not so great for visual unity as they darken dramatically when wet and 'age' quickly outdoors with dirt and algae. Terracotta tiles are cheaper than stone, though neither so hardwearing nor so frost-proof. Terrazzo – stone chippings set in coloured cement – is a glamorous, versatile, but expensive option. But whatever those fancy-pants modern architects might say, ordinary grey concrete (which can be great outdoors) is dull and impractical indoors.

textural contrast

Variety is the spice of life. Just as male and female reflect the best in each other, so rough stone chippings bring out the smoothness of slate and sheet steel, and soft plantings bring hard landscaping alive.

five opposites that attract

1 • rough and smooth

The 'wrong' side of bricks and paving slabs is sometimes 'just right'. Concrete can be laid and left plain, it can be ribbed when on the verge of setting, it can be polished once it's rock hard. Add variety to your garden by revealing the different facets of a single material.

2 • fast and loose

Sturdy slabs lend weight and substance to chippings. Chippings bring lightness and fluidity to stone. Combine the two to stunning effect – and save time, money and labour in the process.

3 • soft and hard

Plants bring inanimate landscaping alive. Grasses add a vertical dimension to floors without impeding progress. Climbers make walls more dynamic. Trees and shrubs bring harmony and discretion to brash and discordant buildings.

4 • natural and manufactured

Raw, organic materials like timber, stone and greenery evoke countryside and wilderness. Paintwork, plastics and metals show the hand of man. A garden is an artificial construct that embraces nature, so play around with the paradox.

5 • ancient and modern

Knotty driftwood fencing, rusted iron plant supports and antique terracotta pots, or freshly cut slats, obelisks of shining steel and funky plastic containers? Why err entirely on one side or the other when you can have the best of both worlds? Youth and age, innocence and experience, call them what you will, there's poignancy in putting them together.

size and scale

Physical appearances aren't as fixed as you might think. They change according to context because the mind's eye is always making comparisons. Exploit this phenomenon wherever you see an opportunity.

it's all in the detail

For example, you can under-scale by growing tiny scrambling ground-cover plants under magnificent, large-leaved foliage plants, by arranging a few small pots or pebbles beside a pool or a large container, or by slipping a delicate fern next to a massive boulder. The small details make the big ones look even more imposing, while the big ones make the small ones even more special.

size matters

Be wary in a small garden of under-scaling to cram more things in. You're not decorating a doll's house. Too much fuss, too many details, and the composition suffers. Here, instead, you should try over-scaling – using a few really large pieces and leaving them plenty of room to breathe. This gives a great sense of luxury and comfort that small gardens often lack. Large leaves, thick stems, giant urns and tall sculptures will give your outdoor space an instant lift.

Or, if you have a favourite plant, then grow it in spreading clumps. Like one material in particular? Use it generously. Sheer physical presence is impressive and thrilling. Don't be coy.

magic circles

Every straight line makes the eye look in one particular direction, but every circle keeps it going around and around, and every meander gives a constant change of direction. Use this knowledge to add magic and mystery to your garden.

five spellbinding tricks

1 • A straight pathway simply takes you there and back, and offers only two views – forwards and backwards, but a circular or serpentine route provides many changes of scenery. And because the walk takes longer, the garden seems bigger and looks better.

2 • On a small balcony or in a courtyard, round tabletops, stone or topiary balls, ceramic pots thrown on a wheel and circular motifs of all kinds hold our eyes in their thrall and give the mind pause for thought.

3 • A circular compartment in a garden – be it gravel edged with box, a circular lawn or a circular paved area – acts as a protective enclosure, a pool of tranquillity, a powerful symbol of security that puts the big wide world at one remove.

4 • A circular dais on a roof terrace encourages you to take in the full 360-degrees view. In the imagination it becomes a crow's nest on a sailing ship, a military observation post, the

the numbers game 20

When it comes to plants, containers or any other decorative feature, the numbers you use dictate the garden's tone. Count on it.

ones

A single bold object is always easy to place. Whether it goes centrally or to the side, the eye understands the power of one.

twos

The simplest way to frame a view, mark an entrance, highlight a bench or a piece of sculpture, or draw attention to a flight of steps is to use matching pots and plants.

threes

Threesomes work anywhere. Try three identical pots, identically planted, or three matching pots in different sizes, differently planted. Or you can try the all-time classic planting combination: something tall and thin, something of medium height with a bit more substance, and something broad that hugs the ground.

fours

Four identical objects instantly delineate a formal space. Sitting areas can be made grander with four potted bay trees; flowerbeds can be smartened up with four standard roses, four box pyramids or four clipped balls of lavender.

odd but true

Large clusters always look better with an odd number. If it's a symmetrical grouping, it needs the addition of a central feature to unite the two mirror images or the composition appears split in half, and if it's an asymmetrical arrangement consisting of an even number of elements, the mind will struggle to find symmetry in it and the result will be discomfort. You'll find that any collection of pots or plants that feels 'wrong' can usually be put 'right' simply by adding an extra element or taking one away.

summit of a mountain. In reality, it's just a bit of raised decking. But, oh, what a view!

5 • To liven up an existing 'square' patio hire someone skilled with an angle-grinder to cut out a circular bed for planting with low-growing succulents. Or add a shallow stone bowl full of water that you can float candles in by night. Circles send out ripples of delight. You and your guests will be truly enchanted.

21

colour in the garden

For some people, a garden wouldn't be a garden without a riot of
flower colour. Others want a garden that's very cool and
disciplined. Chances are that you're after something in between, in
which case, you need to know a bit – only a tiny bit – about the
theory of colour. And it also pays to remember that colour is just
as important in the landscaping materials you use as in the plants
you choose.

theory

The colours of the rainbow run the gamut through red, orange,
yellow, green, blue, indigo and violet. Look closely and you'll see
that the real range is infinite, because each colour turns
imperceptibly to the next. Reds range through magenta, rose,
crimson, carmine, scarlet and vermilion to flame-like orange.
Orange slowly lightens to yellow. Yellows acquire limier,
greener hues. Greens merge into blues. Blues become purples.
Grape and plum purples turn into burgundy reds. Reds . . . you
get the picture.

practice

For relaxed planting schemes choose flower colours that sit close
to each other on the spectrum. Enrich the picture with colour-
related glazed pottery, painted benches, rendered walls, and so on.

eye eye

Our eyes only register three colours: red, yellow and blue – the
'primary' colours. Our brain recognises all the other colours by
their combined impact on the retina. Red and yellow make orange,
yellow and blue make green, blue and red make violet. These are
known as the 'secondary' colours.

see here

For a bit of stimulation, try contrasting one primary colour with the secondary colour made from the other two: red with green (made from blue and yellow), yellow with violet (made from red and blue), blue with orange (made from red and yellow). Each contrast is as far removed as possible from the other on the spectrum, and every sensor in the eye is at work. The effect is dazzling!

remember that . . .

• Colours can be bright and intense, or muted and grey. They come in deep, dark shades or they can be diluted to the lightest of tints. Schemes of many shades and tints of just one colour can be really beguiling.

• Hot colours like red and orange come right at you. Use them to make a long narrow site look shorter. Cool colours like green and blue seem to fade into the distance. They never overpower a small space.

• Wherever there's a relationship, there'll be harmony: pastels always look pretty together; dark materials have a mysterious affinity whatever their hue.

• Colours that clash in theory often look great together outdoors while indoors they could be a disaster. The reason? In the garden they are separated by lots of greenery and fresh air.

• There's no law that says you have to have a colour scheme in your garden at all. A riotous mix of blooms can be a joy. However, if things get out of hand and you'd like a little peace, add some white flowers to calm the rabble down.

• For a really soothing garden simply use white and green. It's a timeless combination that's always in fashion, and it looks great by night.

22 get the look

You're beginning to know what you like . . . but do you really? There's so much to choose from. And once you've chosen, do you know how to translate what you like into what you want to have?

single-minded

Few outdoor spaces can sustain more than one vision. Unless you have a front and a back garden, two separate balconies, or some other means of demarcation, you'll need to choose a single style and stick to it.

small but essential

Small gardens must state their case succinctly. You can't have a prairie on a rooftop or a jungle in a courtyard. You must capture their essence instead.

find the key

What is it about your source of inspiration that really strikes a chord? Think hard. For example, an English country estate might contain billowing flowerbeds, a topiary parterre, elaborate stonework, a vast expanse of water. Which key element do you most want at home? Choose it. Then use it.

be bold

Have the courage of your convictions: whatever the size of your garden always work on a grand scale; begin with a bold statement then repeat your leitmotif with themes and variations – like Mozart or Wagner, not like a schoolchild tootling on the recorder.

lateral thinking

You can't always have the genuine article, so you'll need to improvise. Some hardy large-leaved plants look incredibly tropical. Ivy and clematis can stand in for rainforest vines. Mediterranean seas and skies don't travel round the world in a suitcase, but you can evoke them with brilliant blue parasols, sun-bleached paint effects on furniture, and white or ochre render on walls.

5 ideas

23 formal attire

Formal gardens are built upon order and symmetry, both in the layout of space and in the plants that fill it. Start with a rectangle, a circle or a square. It doesn't matter if the boundaries of your garden are irregular just so long as you work from the inside of your garden outwards. Aim for a great view from your home, and close the vista with something spectacular such as a large urn, or piece of sculpture.

Topiary is an absolute must, as it clearly shows the hand of man. Roses trained as standards are another triumph of art over nature. Use bedding plants en masse at ground level as they can be bought in at the peak of perfection then replaced at will. Historically, formal gardens always had a wilderness, an informal 'wild' area that provided contrast. Keep the tradition alive by filling odd planting pockets around the perimeter with billowing perennials, wall shrubs and climbers.

key features
- Order and symmetry
- Rectangles, circles and squares
- Axes and vistas
- Topiary
- Statuary

key plants
- Boxwood, bay trees, yew
- Roses, lavender, santolina
- Tulips
- Massed biennials
- Brightly coloured annuals for summer bedding

country casuals

The higgledy-piggledy look is one of the easiest to achieve, but the cottage garden's reliance on summer blooms can make it a rather sorry sight in winter.

Ornaments and hard landscaping should have a mellow careworn feel: salvaged chimneypots, crumbly bricks, reclaimed stone and old copper washtubs are ideal.

Buy flowering annuals and perennials of as many different heights and habits as you can, and choose highly scented varieties wherever possible. Fill every nook and cranny with self-seeders such as lady's mantle (*Alchemilla mollis*), heartsease (*Viola tricolor*) and evening primrose (*Oenothera biennis*). You never know where they'll pop up next.

key features
- Crowded, full-to-bursting planting
- Weathered brick and stone
- Old-looking ornaments
- Scented flowers
- Lots of colour

five essential annuals
1 • Snapdragons (*Antirrhinum majus*)
2 • Night-scented stocks (*Matthiola bicornis*)
3 • Love-in-a-mist (*Nigella damascena*)
4 • Field poppy (*Papaver rhoeas*)
5 • Nasturtiums (*Tropaeolum majus*)

five essential biennials
1 • Hollyhocks (*Alcea rosea*)
2 • Foxgloves (*Digitalis purpurea*)
3 • Wallflowers (*Erysimum cheiri*)
4 • Honesty (*Lunaria annua*)
5 • Forget-me-nots (*Myosotis sylvatica*)

five essential perennials
1 • Japanese anemones (*Anemone* x *hybrida*)
2 • Columbine (*Aquilegia vulgaris*)
3 • Bleeding heart (*Dicentra spectabilis*)
4 • Purple coneflower (*Echinacea purpurea*)
5 • Cranesbill (*Geranium* 'Johnson's Blue')

grass roots

Grasses are enormously versatile. They come into their own where only a few plants are to be used, where low maintenance is a requirement, and where year-round good looks are paramount. Their elegant leaves, wiry stems and delicate seed heads work sympathetically with such materials as concrete, steel and glass, while their muted palette of greens and yellows, glaucous blues, warm reds and soft browns means that they also blend well with brick, old stonework, rusted metal and weathered wood.

Grasses also have clear graphic outlines, fill a space while having little actual substance, rustle and flutter in the gentlest of breezes, tolerate poor soil and drought and look great in pots.

Their new growth looks incredibly fresh in spring, many are evergreen, and many that turn brown in autumn have elegant winter silhouettes. Looking their most beautiful when backlit by the evening sun, they are ideal for balconies and roof gardens, but the long and the short of it is that grasses look great everywhere. Why not base your entire garden design around them?

six of the best

1 • *Carex comans* bronze   Long and flowing auburn tresses
2 • *Cyperus eragrostis*   Strange and papyrus-like
3 • *Festuca glauca*   Spiky metallic blue hummocks
4 • *Imperata cylindrica* 'Rubra'   Ruby-red new growth
5 • *Panicum virgatum* 'Heavy Metal'   Steely and erect
6 • *Phalaris arundinacea* 'Picta'   Dashing white stripes

minimalist chic

Is a minimalist garden just an empty space? NO
So it's more about elegance and simplicity? YES
Then it works well in modern apartments? ABSOLUTELY
Using architectural plants and containers? ALWAYS IN MODERATION
But how does it work in a garden setting? THEN IT CAN BECOME EXPENSIVE
Because you need high quality materials? YES
Is there an affordable alternative to this? REALLY EXQUISITE PLANTS
Like narrow-stemmed trees or bamboos? PRECISELY
Instead of the expected hard landscaping? YES
So, a softer approach for a gentler place? A+

ten key features

stone, glass, steel, concrete and render / space treated as element of design / emphatic verticals and horizontals / continuous planes as boundary walls / over-scaled slabs for steps and flooring / matching, massive, built-in furniture / clean lines, square edges / sharp corners / no curves except occasional circular arcs / architectural links between indoors and out / stone chippings used to mulch bare earth

ten key plants

1 • *Acanthus spinosus*   6 • *Echinops ritro*
2 • *Achillea millefolium*   7 • *Euphorbia characias*
3 • *Agapanthus africanus*   8 • *Iris pallida*
4 • *Allium cristophii*   9 • *Melianthus major*
5 • *Cynara cardunculus*   10 • *Phyllostachys nigra*

brute force

27

Urban spaces can be edgy and uncompromising. That's all part of the appeal of warehouse and factory conversions, and of purpose-built developments in tough inner-city areas. Flues and drainpipes, ducts and cabling, skylights and fire escapes might all be on show. The surrounding view might include a flyover, a railway bridge, a factory and more than a few office blocks.

If you create a garden that's too elaborate or if you try to screen off your surroundings, what you're saying in effect is 'Help! Get me out of here!' This doesn't make for a very comfortable space. Not only that, your garden will be so out of keeping with the immediate environment that it will be the blot on the landscape.

Get streetwise. Use rough-and-ready landscaping materials and stocky little plants that can fend for themselves. Adopt the local vocabulary by using galvanised drums and concrete pots, by sitting on chairs of wire mesh, by making tables and railings from scaffolding poles.

ten edgy plants

1 • *Corokia cotoneaster*
2 • *Eryngium variifolium*
3 • *Hebe canterburiensis* 'Prostrata'
4 • *Helianthemum apenninum*
5 • *Ophiopogon planiscapus* 'Nigrescens'
6 • *Penstemon pinifolius*
7 • *Saxifraga stribrnyi*
8 • *Sedum spathulifolium* 'Cape Blanco'
9 • *Sedum telephium*
10 • *Thymus vulgaris*

siesta

In botanical and climatic terms, 'Mediterranean' means anywhere with cool winters and warm dry summers. So besides all the countries that actually border the Mediterranean Sea, the term includes places like Australia, California, the Canary Islands, Chile and South Africa. Take global warming into account, and anyone in Northern Europe or North America with a sunny site and well-drained soil that doesn't freeze too hard in winter can count themselves in, too.

key features

• Brilliant or chalky blue, clean bright white, sun-bleached pink and warm ochre are the most evocative colours. Use them on walls and fencing, for sunshades and for furniture.

• Use as many real Mediterranean shrubs, climbers and perennials as your climate will allow. For the rest, use native lookalikes that echo their shapes and colours. Fill any gaps with bright summer bedding.

• Use containers such as Greek pithoi, French or Italian glazed terracotta or the colourfully painted wares of Spain and Portugal.

• Build yourself a great barbecue, and grow herbs like rosemary and thyme close by.

twenty plants that say it all

1 • agapanthus
2 • asphodel
3 • bougainvillea
4 • cistus
5 • cupressus
6 • echium
7 • eleagnus
8 • fig
9 • grape vine
10 • lavender
11 • marguerite
12 • melianthus
13 • mesembryanthemum
14 • mimosa
15 • myrtle
16 • nerium
17 • olive
18 • osteospermum
19 • pelargonium
20 • yucca

japanese style

Japanese gardens evoke feelings of stillness and security. Their deeper symbolic meanings might be lost on Occidentals but they still provide a focus for contemplation and meditation – and they're a never-ending source of inspiration.

different gardens for different things

Gravel gardens represent selected aspects of nature in a few well-considered brushstrokes. Tea gardens are about retreat and ritual purification. Stroll gardens with winding paths and shifting viewpoints encompass all of creation.

key pointers

10 ideas

Asymmetry reveals natural order rather than the artifice of civilisation. Careful positioning of rocks, ornaments and plants creates a narrative structure. Whether a garden is to be walked through or to be traversed only by the eye, 'flow' is an essential element.

the world in miniature

One tree in a garden can symbolise a whole forest or you can have a miniature wood of bonsai in a shallow earthenware bowl. A few rocks can stand in for an entire mountain range. This philosophy translates beautifully into tiny courtyards and small balconies the whole world over.

get rockin'

Rocks can be tall or short uprights with vertical strata suggesting waterfalls, they can recline like resting human figures, they can bob jauntily like a boat on a river, or they can be flat, solid and grounded. Rugged angular pieces suggest craggy mountainsides, rounded boulders look as if they've been washed smooth by water. Rocks can tell countless stories and evoke a strong sense of place. Sink them at least one-third into the ground for visual balance. Consider using fibreglass rocks on balconies and roof gardens.

stone and gravel

Water-worn pebbles can be used to create 'dry' riverbeds – lay them as though they've tumbled into place under the influence of a strong current. Create ripples, waves and swirls of water in beds of gravel or crushed stone using a coarse-toothed wooden rake.

water

Though hard landscaping materials alone often suggest its presence, real water can be introduced either with a stone basin or a finely balanced bamboo deer scarer that clacks hard upon a stone on emptying. Though traditionally filled with diverted stream or spring water, a re-circulating pump (see 72) does the job just as well.

ornament

Traditional artefacts include lanterns in stone or bronze, statues of Buddha and miniature pagodas. These are all precious objects that should be used with reverence and restraint.

trees

Evergreen, small-leaved trees such as pines work well in a Japanese-style garden. They look ruggedly mature even

when young and can be pruned to scale and trained to look windswept.

- *Cryptomeria japonica* Japanese cedar
- *Pinus contorta* beach pine
- *Pinus densiflora* Japanese red pine
- *Pinus parviflora* Japanese white pine

Of the deciduous trees, consider cherries and apricots for spring blossom, and the many varieties of Japanese maple (*Acer palmatum*) and the gingko (*Gingko biloba*), for autumn colour.

shrubs

For their blooms, grow *Camellia japonica*, *Chaenomeles japonica*, *Hamamelis japonica*, *Mahonia japonica* and small-flowered rhododendron species like *R. luteum* (the botanists won't let us call them azaleas anymore). Grow *Aucuba japonica*, *Euonymus japonicus*, *Ligustrum japonicum*, *Fatsia japonica* and *Pieris japonica* for their foliage. Add some graceful bamboos to add sound and movement when the wind blows.

ground cover

Specially cultivated 'turves' of moss are sold in Japan but see 37 for some practical substitutes you can use in other parts of the world.

30 tropical paradise

You don't have to live in the Brazilian rainforest to stage a tropical or subtropical show in your garden. Take Hollywood, not the atlas, as your guide.

the script
- Use evocative hard landscaping
- Choose decorative details that reinforce your theme
- Chance your hardier subtropicals in the ground
- Develop an imaginative framework of perennials
- Over-winter really delicate species in your home

the set
- Raised decking walkways
- Sawn logs as paving
- Boundaries masked by climbers
- Water for dramatic reflections and humidity

the decoration
- Introduce colour using tiles, mosaics and paint
- Buy a tree-fern carving or some 'primitive' art
- Choose bamboo furniture, gates and fence panels
- Install a pair of 'antique' temple doors

the movie stars
Coddle these through the winter as your climate directs and they'll give a great performance each summer.

- *Musa basjoo* The Japanese banana is one of the hardiest. Wrap it up in horticultural fleece or sacking whenever frosts threaten.
- *Canna* The leaves can be green, green and yellow or purple-brown. Flowers come in yellow, orange and red, or in combinations of all three. Protect the crowns in winter with a thick dry mulch.

the supporting actors
- *Astelia chathamica*
- *Aucuba japonica* 'Crotonifolia'
- *Cordyline australis* 'Albertii'
- *Fatsia japonica* 'Variegata'
- *Gunnera manicata*
- *Hedera hibernica* 'Deltoidea'
- *Phormium tenax* 'Dazzler'
- *Rheum palmatum*
- *Rodgersia pinnata* 'Superba'
- *Trachycarpus fortunei*

the extras
Many houseplants are rainforest natives and like a summer holiday outdoors – but out of scorching sun.

- *Alocasia*
- *Asparagus densiflorus*
- *Aspidistra*
- *Chlorophytum comosum*
- *Monstera deliciosa*
- *Philodendron*
- *Sparmannia africana*

in the shade

In hot countries a cool shady place is a coveted spot, a welcome retreat from the heat of the sun. Darkness and seclusion evoke powerful spiritual and emotional responses – night and day, good and evil. Turn any unloved, light-forsaken space you've got into a personal sanctuary.

get away with murder!

In poor light, you can get away with substitute materials.
- Concrete slabs are far cheaper than stone.
- Black plastic pots blend into the background.
- Fake terracotta is far harder to detect.

enhance the mood

What you haven't got in colour you can make up for in decorative effects.
- Use mirrors imaginatively (see 46).
- Install a bubbling or gently trickling water feature.
- Use candles or fairy lights by night.

ten top plants

1 • Hart's tongue fern (*Asplenium scolopendrium*)
2 • Blue fumitory (*Corydalis flexuosa*)
3 • Barrenwort (*Epimedium acuminatum*)
4 • Plantain lily (*Hosta*)
5 • Rose of Sharon (*Hypericum calycinum*)
6 • Dead nettle (*Lamium maculatum*)
7 • Lilyturf (*Liriope muscari*)
8 • Shuttlecock fern (*Matteuccia struthiopteris*)
9 • Piggyback plant (*Tolmeia menziesii* 'Taff's Gold')
10 • Greater periwinkle (*Vinca major*)

eclectic style

A garden can be eccentric and intensely personal. If you have the eye of a collector or admire theatrical effects, you will constantly be resetting the scene. Give your imagination free rein, but weed old things out as you tire of them.

• Wirework plant stands and furniture have an idiosyncratic charm. Metal gates and grilles can be wall-mounted as decorative trelliswork. Old pub and shop signs can be used to witty effect. Salvage yards and junk shops are great sources of inspiration.

• See what you can buy at jumble sales or flea markets, even what you can find in skips: put pots of trailing flowers in old birdcages; give rattan chairs a quick paint job with a spray can; adopt a dressmaker's mannequin.

• Then, with the money you've saved, be wildly extravagant: buy a carved statue, hang up an old chandelier, backlight a stained glass window.

five key plants

These entrancing but demanding prima donnas will keep you on your toes.
1 • *Cobaea scandens*
2 • *Gloriosa superba* 'Rothschildiana'
3 • *Passiflora* 'Incense'
4 • *Strelitzia reginae*
5 • *Zantedeschia aethiopica* 'Green Goddess'

part two

getting down to the detail

33 ground rules

You just need to follow a few simple ground rules to be sure of the ground under your feet.

eyes down

Don't take your garden floor for granted. Just as we breathe without thinking, so we constantly cast our eyes to the ground as we walk. If we didn't we'd fall over! Since you can't help but look at it, you owe it to yourself to make the earth beneath your feet as beautiful as possible.

waste not want not

Something can always be done to improve what you've already got. A good scrub or a blast from a power hose works wonders on grubby stone, concrete and brick; re-pointing really revitalises. Decking can be sanded and re-stained; sometimes the planks can be lifted and re-laid upside down. Lawns can be weeded, raked free of moss and then fertilised; bare patches can always be reseeded.

drainage

Efficient drainage is essential as lingering rainwater makes surfaces slippery and treacherous. Besides leading to accidents, it can also cause long-term structural damage. It can rot and discolour decking or, as it freezes and expands, it can make brick and concrete paviours crumble or crack in winter. A barely discernible slope of just 1 in 60 will ensure adequate runoff. If there isn't an area of garden soil for water to soak away into you should direct it to a drain.

damp-proof

Surfaces that butt up to any building should lie well below its damp-proof course. Don't jeopardise the structure of your home! It is common practice for successive owners to lay new slabs on old or to add fresh layers of concrete. Slowly, slowly the ground level rises, and closer and closer comes the risk of rising damp.

cost-effective

Popular routes around the garden and places where people sit require practical, durable surfaces that stand up to wear and tear. The materials for these tend to be expensive but areas that only experience occasional footfall can be given softer, looser and, yes! cheaper treatments. By using a variety of materials you create patterns that lead people naturally to places of interest. You also stand to save money, and you can do each bit of work at a time – which means you don't have to pay for everything at once.

budget

In a really small space the cost of new groundworks can be negligible and you may well be able to do the work yourself. But the costs quickly escalate the larger the area involved – a 2m x 2m square of any surfacing material will cost four times as much as 1m x 1m square. So think the job through carefully, always check whether the price you are quoted includes tax, allow for unseen materials like rubble for foundations and joists for decking, and also allow for transportation, the purchase or hire of tools, and for specialist help. Finally, add on a contingency fund of at least 10 per cent of the overall cost.

labour

Where a good finish is essential, it pays to use an experienced builder or landscaper; hiring second-rate workmen is a false economy. Save money if you like by acting as a labourer; you get to keep an eye on things and it's a great way of acquiring new skills. And if you are doing the work yourself you might consider calling in a friend or two, just so long as you're prepared to return the favour one day.

testing, testing

Showroom samples help you narrow down your choice, but they can be misleading. Stone and wood in particular are subject to a great deal of natural variation, so to get a real idea of what you're buying you need to go out into the stockyard. Look at flooring materials close up to assess their quality, take a bottle of water so you can check out how dark they turn when wet, and finally, ask for as large a sample as possible and take it home to assess it in situ.

compatibility counts

All the materials you use should look great together in the garden, and they should also look attractive from indoors. If appropriate, check too that they sit well against your property when they are viewed from the street.

spares and repairs

Accidents happen. Materials will only match perfectly if you buy them all at the same time, from the same source. Allow a small margin of error when ordering in, and keep a few leftovers if you can. If ever you have to replace a weathered slab, a paviour or a decking plank in a highly visible spot, there's a professional secret well worth knowing: move an old one in from the sidelines, and replace that piece with the new one.

10 ideas

34 rough and ready

Loose-lay surfaces come in a wide range of colours and are the easiest of all to install. Just slice open a bag and pour them into place. Easy! However, bear in mind that small chippings can wander indoors on the soles of your shoes and damage household flooring.

gravel

Naturally occurring gravel is sifted and graded into particles of different sizes. Fine grades are the easiest to walk on, larger stones slow you down as they scrunch underfoot. Weed-proof membranes tend to make you slip and slide, so for areas of heavy use consider having an underlay of compacted hardcore instead and keep weeds down with a rake.

crushed stone

Made by grinding quarry waste, every particle is from the same parent stone, so the colour is uniform throughout. Compared to the rounded particles of gravel, crushed stone is sharp-edged and matt-finished.

tumbled slate

Shards of slate in colours ranging from grey to green whose edges have been tumbled smooth make attractive ground cover but they are the devil to walk on. Because the pieces are quite large they read well visually and look great around areas of decking. Slate also glistens beautifully after rainfall.

pulverised bark

It's no fun at all to fall onto stone chippings with bare arms or legs. If you have children, then pulverised bark is a kinder alternative. If you've just moved into a newly built house it can be laid all over the garden as both a temporary surface and a long-term soil improver. As you develop your garden, perhaps putting in a lawn and some paving, so the pulverised bark slowly turns into humus and disappears from view.

35 all hands on deck

Decking has long been popular in North America and Australia, but is now rightly popular in much of Europe, too. It is relatively easy to install and brings the natural beauty of wood to the most urban of spaces.

five plus points

1 • Decking is an imaginative approach to disguising surfaces that are way past their best. Compare the cost of decking with the expense of digging up and removing old concrete or tarmac. You'll be pleasantly surprised.

2 • Building a deck is the easiest way of creating a large level area on an awkwardly sloping site.

3 • Timber is lightweight and easy to manoeuvre, especially readily available decking squares, so it's perfect for installing on balconies and roof gardens.

4 • Quality hardwoods mellow to silver-grey with age and tone beautifully with plants and buildings alike.

5 • Inexpensive softwoods require a soak-in preservative to keep them sound. Make a virtue of this by using colour stains to add drama.

five hot tips

1 • Rough-sawn or machine-grooved planks give a good grip underfoot when they are new but harbour dirt and water that will lead to slime. In the long term, smooth-sawn timbers are best.

2 • For strength and stability the boards need to be laid crosswise over a framework of joists, so decide well in advance which direction you'd like them to go. Walkways look more dynamic when they run in the direction of movement. Platforms are more relaxed spaces, so slats that are perpendicular to your main line of vision give pause for thought.

3 • Leave a gap between each slat to allow for air circulation, drainage, and for the expansion and contraction of the wood.

4 • Guard against rust by using solid brass or stainless-steel screws. If you're using a resinous wood like cedar then stainless steel is essential.

5 • The odd trap door can stop a children's sandpit from becoming a litter tray, can hide a stash of tools, flowerpots and compost, or give ready access to a manhole cover.

lawns

Fresh, green and soft, small lawns are easy to keep in trim.

easy

An area that's a comfortable size for sunbathing will need nothing more than a strimmer or a pair of hand shears to keep its height in check.

beautiful

A circle or a square surrounded by bricks or paving will always keep its shape but if you want a greater choice, go for islands of grass among gravel or other sorts of chippings (see 34). Hold everything in place with metal edging strips.

blooming

Whatever size of lawn you choose, it will look great smothered with small springtime bulbs like crocus. Once flowering is over, their leaves disappear without a trace. Pop in a whole sackful after levelling the ground but before sowing seed or laying turf.

cheap

When you're starting from scratch, remember that even the very finest seed is incredibly cheap. Avoid all the hassle of watering by sowing in early spring or autumn. To hit the ground running, buy pre-germinated seed but for instant results, lay turf.

cop out

And if all that sounds too much for you, use astroturf – almost all the fun and none of the hassle.

grass substitutes

Where looks are paramount and foot traffic is minimal, these five ground-hugging plants make breathtaking lawns and look great amongst paving. Several are scented so there'll be no keeping you off the 'grass'.

1 • *Chamaemelum nobile*
Chamomile's soft feathery leaves release the scent of ripe green apples when crushed. 'Treneague' is a non-flowering form especially suitable for lawns.

2 • *Mentha requienii*
The creeping stems of Corsican mint root as they go to give dense, tight leaf cover. The pale lilac flowers that appear in summer look really beautiful in the shady places this plant likes best.

3 • *Sagina subulata*
Irish moss is a great cushion plant for flowing between rocks and stone slabs in Japanese gardens. Left to its own devices it forms lovely plump hummocks.

4 • *Soleirolia soleiroleii*
Mind-your-own-business is very invasive indeed given dampish shade. Its translucent stems and tiny round leaves belie its ox-like constitution. Depend on it for greenery in difficult sites.

5 • *Thymus serpyllum*
Mat-forming thymes release their fragrance when stepped on, and give you whorls of white, pink or purple flowers in summer. Choose a dry sunny spot and trim them close to the ground each spring.

38

concrete poetry

Concrete was used by the ancient Egyptians and the Romans, and now it's enjoying a well-deserved renaissance. Here's why.

fluidity

Concrete is a boon in awkward enclosed spaces where bricks or slabs would have to be cut with precision, and where they would draw attention to irregularities. Concrete takes awkward corners and uneven walls in its stride: all you see is a seamless expanse of floor.

colour

Concrete can be dyed. Forget about those red and yellow sunburst patios of the seventies. Think instead of the rich dark browns of expensive leather, of soft charcoals, warm greys and mellow ochres. Très chic!

form

There are now precast slabs that look like York stone paving but come at a fraction of the price. Small tessellating paviours add a touch of modernity.

texture

Poured concrete can be polished smooth, it can be brushed to expose the aggregate, it can be impressed with leaves, flowers and bamboo canes that you later remove to create enigmatic 'fossil' remains, or it can be embossed with the grain of rough-sawn timber floated over the top.

versatility

Precast slabs aren't the only option. Achieve a really interesting effect by casting slabs in situ to any size you want using simple wooden frames as moulds on a base of compacted hardcore. Knock away the frames when the concrete is fully set and fill the gaps between your new slabs with gravel, glass beads or a low-growing ground cover.

39

the best laid plans

When it comes to other underfoot surfaces for your garden, use your imagination – nothing's set in stone!

bricks

Laying bricks is a skilled and back-breaking task that's best handed over to professionals, but choosing a sympathetic colour and deciding on the pattern they're laid in is down to you.

stone slabs

These can be fixed into place on a bed of wet mortar, atop five stiff dabs, or settled onto a layer of dry sand and cement. In a really informal garden they can simply be laid on levelled earth.

multimedia

Concrete, brick or stone are classic partners, but there are plenty more materials to play around with.
- concrete ammonites
- granite or porphyry setts
- industrial cogs
- metal grids and grilles
- railway sleepers
- sawn logs

40

level-headed

Look on a change of level in the garden as a nuisance and you'll end up with some boring way of dealing with it. Regard it instead as an opportunity to create a feature.

- Garden steps and stairways must be wider and shallower than their indoor equivalents. They're not just a means of getting from A to B, they're an end in themselves.
- As you ascend or descend a staircase your perspective changes. It's great to be able to stand still and admire the view from every level. Deep treads do the business.
- Grow trailing plants alongside the steps to blur their edges. These eat into the walking space, which is why you need breadth.
- Steps make perfect staging for containers. Repeats of strong architectural evergreens lend rhythm and substance. Once again, they take up room.
- The more precipitous the steps, the more important a side rail. Besides offering physical assistance, handgrips are psychologically reassuring.
- In an ideal world, a long flight of steps would have a landing every sixth riser. Besides providing a great vantage point, landings help break falls, providing built-in safety for children, old people and anyone in a hurry.
- Neither steps nor stairs should ever get slippery when wet. Cast iron grilles, rough brick, and textured concrete or stone make ideal steps. Watch out for wood, though.
- Signpost the top of a stairway with matching pairs of plants, pots or ornaments.
- Ensure that there is nothing sharp to fall onto at the bottom.
- If you or a great many of your guests are elderly or infirm then consider installing a ramp. Your stairway to heaven will come in God's own time.

41 boundary issues

The closer we live to our neighbours, the more we guard our territory and the more importance we attach to our privacy. What we can't achieve by keeping our distance we impose with a barrier, and curiously, its height and impenetrability is generally in inverse proportion to the size of the garden. That is why walls and fences between small town gardens tend to be higher and more solid than those in large gardens, where clipped evergreen hedges generally prevail. It's why rambling country gardens rarely have more than a simple open fence or informal mixed hedging, and why great estates merge seamlessly into the surrounding countryside.

the good

• There is an exciting variety of natural and man-made materials on offer.
• Attractive boundaries and internal partitions add colour and drama and can become great garden backdrops.
• Enlivened with flowering shrubs and climbers they become gardens in their own right. Retaining walls create whole new planting areas.

the bad

• The taller and more obscure the boundary, the further-reaching and denser the shade it casts.
• A 'rain shadow' can leave the soil at its base permanently parched.
• Where does reasonable privacy end and claustrophobia begin?

the ugly

• Walls are incredibly expensive to build. If you've already got one but it's a bit dilapidated then give it a facelift (see 43)
• Ready-made, mass-market fencing needn't be ruled out, it can always be customised (see 44) What you can't improve upon, you can always disguise with greenery.

gentle restraint 42

The higher up a building you are the more you're shielded from sight and the more you get to spy on everyone else, so the greater part of dealing with balcony and rooftop boundaries isn't about privacy, it's about optimising the view. The boundary itself is a given; whether it's sheer glass, solid brick or grandiose stone it's an integral part of the building. The treatment you give it is what counts.

glass

This gives you solid protection from the wind and a totally unobstructed view. Out of respect for the architectural integrity of the building, keep plants towards the back wall and put stylish clean-lined seating close towards the front – blue or white reads best from ground level.

railings

Containers all in a row look great right up against the edge: the secondary barrier they create is psychologically reassuring, and trailing plants can cascade down between the uprights.

balustrades

A few generously scaled pots look best, preferably in the same material as the balusters, which are generally of cast stone. Imitation stone planters in plastic or fibreglass are a cheaper, more manoeuvrable alternative; wooden Versailles planters are a smart way of introducing some contrast.

parapets

Low solid walls are usually the preserve of roof gardens or older-style balconies. Use them as backdrops for tableaux to be viewed as much as anything from indoors. Consider a Japanese approach (see 29).

walls 43

Building a wall is a job for a skilled professional, but you can keep costs down by acting as the brickie's labourer.

stone

Stone is natural and beautiful, but usually too expensive for enclosing walls. But as an edge for raised beds, it is magnificent and affordable. Opt for local stone: it's the cheapest and will also be in sympathy with your immediate environment.

brick

If your house is built of brick, then aim for a perfect match both with regard to the bricks and how they are laid. Alternatively, use a more rustic brick for the wall itself but matching brick for the supporting piers and for capping off the top.

concrete and glass

Use modern materials for walls with a twist. Try pierced concrete blocks – retro chic has made them fashionable again. Consider glass bricks too – they're clear enough to allow light in, obscure enough to shield your neighbours from view.

a new lease of life

Old brick walls can be re-pointed. Ugly old walls can be painted. Use a breathable limewash or exterior-grade masonry paint and stick to pale earth tones. Chance your arm on a more vibrant colour and the worst you'll have to do is repaint.

fences 44

Cheap as chips, attractive and practical, traditional or cutting edge, you can always find a fence to suit your pocket and to match your style.

choose it

Chain-link fencing is a cheap way to mark a boundary while establishing a hedge.

- Ready-made lapped, woven and close-board wooden panels are garden-centre staples.
- Marine ply can be cut to size by timber merchants.
- Simple picket fences can be constructed from old planks or floorboards and have an old-world charm.
- Post-and-rail fencing looks great in open countryside.
- Palisades of cedar driftwood look great by the sea.
- Japanese bamboo fences lend an air of instant calm.
- For rusticity choose woven hurdles in hazel and willow.
- Specialist suppliers mail out lengths of living willow in spring and autumn. Stick them in the ground, weave in a few horizontal supports and let Nature do the rest.
- Corrugated steel is edgy and urban – it can be zinc-galvanised or powder-coated in a wide range of colours

customise it

- A finial atop each fencepost raises the tone of any garden in a trice.
- If you have upright slats, use an electric saw to cut an upwards curve along the top edge of the panels for an arcade effect or a downwards curve for a garland effect. The panels' strength is unaffected.
- Strong but plain fences can be masked with fencing rolls made of willow, heather brushwood, peeled reed or split bamboo.

don't just sit on it

45 trellising

Trellising is a lightweight and decorative way to raise the height of a garden fence for added privacy and security while still letting light through. Burglars hate it because it won't hold their weight. Plants on the other hand, love to climb right through it.

Trellising around a roof garden helps protect both you and your plants from the wind. It also gives a satisfying sense of privacy without totally obscuring the view. You can screen out whatever you don't want to see, and where there's a good vantage point you can frame it like a picture by cutting out a porthole or a window.

keep an open mind

• Trelliswork is usually made from stained or painted wood, but woven strips of copper or aluminium, and bamboo poles lashed firmly together are exciting alternatives.
• Besides square lattices consider diamonds or oriental motifs. Mix and match in different panels.

be practical

If you're making your own, remember that you're outdoors: too precise a join, too fine a tolerance, and it'll all warp or split in the damp or in the heat. You need tough, practical carpentry that can adapt itself to the elements.

a vehicle for colour

Trellising provides great contrast in front of a wall. Try white against a pale chalky green for a relaxing expansive effect, or dark green against brick red for something altogether more imposing.

46 they do it with mirrors

Panels of reflective glass or plastic open up all kinds of possibilities for illusion and duplicity.

one

To make a drab or ugly boundary wall dissolve into thin air you can cover it with a mirror and put trellis on top. In a shady, subterranean garden, the reflected light from the mirror helps plants to grow, and gives the illusion of a view through the trellis. Alternatively, if there's something beautiful to reflect, you can leave the glass completely plain to give a greater sense of depth.

two

For a tantalising glimpse of 'another' garden, fix a door with its frame to a wall, slip a mirror into the frame and leave the door slightly ajar. This gives a very real feeling that you could open the door at any moment and walk into something rather marvellous beyond. Not only do your surroundings become so much more attractive, your territory appears suddenly to have doubled.

three

To keep the fantasy intact, try to blur mirrors at eye level with plants and ornaments so that people aren't challenged by their own reflections.

47
murals

A mural on a brick or render wall or even on a shed adds a whole new dimension to any garden. Look to a favourite plant for inspiration or turn to art – try a naive jungle scene in the style of le Douanier Rousseau, or abstract blocks of colour. You could have an artist paint the mural for you, but why not have a go yourself? It's easier than you might think.

• Prime the surface before painting on a background colour.
• Use a slide projector or an overhead projector to cast your image or design upon the wall then draw the outlines in charcoal or in watery white paint.
• Alternatively, plot a small grid on a paper pattern and a much larger one on the wall. With the squares as a guide you can scale up the design freehand.
• Be bold, confident and generous. Don't worry about details, think and work in broad brushstrokes.
• Use exterior-grade paint. You don't want your masterpiece washed away.

48
trompe l'œil

real . . .

You need a high degree of artistry with paint or mosaic to fool the eye, but the results can be phenomenal: a sunny skyline, a prospect of lavender fields through an archway, a statue in an alcove, or a fishpond you can walk on. These are just a few tiny miracles to consider.

. . . or fake, like this artful cloud-studded sky?

mosaic 49

Mosaics appeal on many levels. Close up, the raw materials themselves can be fascinating. A little further away, we admire the skill and patience that goes into their composition. At a greater distance still, everything melds into a unified picture or design. Mosaics can be executed on walls and hanging plaques, on floors and tables, on pots and statuary – in fact on almost any hard surface in the garden.

1 • materials

glass Venetian smalti are tiny hand-clipped pieces of coloured glass that really sparkle. Larger glass tiles about 1cm square are easier and cheaper for beginners to work with, as are those flattened glass beads that look like children's sweets. Handled with care, broken bottle glass can look really beautiful, but the range of colours is rather limited. Mirror glass looks fantastic in the sun.

stone Professionals use tesserae of coloured marble and semi-precious stones like lapis, serpentine and malachite. Amateurs will find that pebbles are cheaper and give faster results, but they are so heavy that their uses are limited to inset wall panels and flooring.

ceramic Broken tiles and crockery are easy to come by and great fun to work with. Ask nicely at your local bathroom store and you'll get free cast-offs. Charity shops and jumble sales are good sources of colourful china and earthenware.

2 • techniques

direct Lay your pieces directly into wet cement or a cement-based adhesive. Foolproof.

reverse For a really smooth and level surface, glue the pieces face down onto strong brown paper with flour-and-water paste. Then press the finished, dried work onto a wet cement bed. When everything is fully hardened, wash away the paper and paste.

3 • finishing touch

grout Mix a frost-proof and waterproof grout according to the manufacturer's instructions. Spread it into all the gaps and wipe away any excess with a barely damp cloth.

50 climbers

Whether they hold on with suckers or tendrils, whether they need a helping hand with trellising or discreet horizontal wires, climbers have an essential role to play in every garden. They soften and disguise unattractive boundaries, they give old and mellow walls a whole new lease of life, they add the perfect finishing touch to beautiful new fences. Mix deciduous plants with evergreens for year-round interest, and for instant effect use fast-growing annuals while perennials get established.

the magnificent seven

1 • *Actinidia kolomikta* grows very pretty leaves that seem to have been dipped first into white paint, then into pink. Its tiny flowers have a lily-of-the-valley scent.

2 • *Clematis armandii* thrives in shade. It has long, glossy evergreen leaves and a profusion of vanilla-scented springtime flowers.

3 • *Hydrangea petiolaris* has clinging aerial roots, requires no pruning, produces white lace-cap flower clusters early in summer, and has leaves that turn yellow in autumn. Gorgeous.

4 • *Ipomoea tricolor* 'Heavenly Blue' is a truly outstanding morning glory that romps away in summer. Grow this tender annual from seed or buy young plants from garden centres in late spring.

5 • *Jasminum nudiflorum* has whippy green stems that are bright with star-like yellow flowers from winter to spring. It is as happy in shade as in full sun.

6 • *Lathyrus latifolius* is a perennial sweet pea that ranges in colour from white through pink to mauve.

7 • *Vitis coignetiae* is a vine with gigantic heart-shaped leaves that turn all shades of yellow, orange, red and brown and purple before falling in autumn.

wall shrubs

A great many shrubs can be grown up house and boundary walls. For optimum impact don't use plants to obscure boundaries completely. It's more telling to use them for colour contrast and architectural effect.

when you're up against it

• *Ceanothus* has both evergreen and deciduous forms, and many named varieties. The powder-blue flower clusters are breathtaking.

• *Chaenomeles*, the Japanese quince, bears apple-blossom flowers in spring that range in colour from white and pink through apricot and orange to brightest red. The fruits resemble crab apples and ripen to golden yellow.

• *Clerodendrum bungei* is a suckering shrub with intensely fragrant pink blooms that are a delight from late summer to early autumn.

• *Itea ilicifolia* sports outrageously long honey-scented catkins in late summer given a sheltered, slightly shady spot.

• *Fremontedendron californicum* grows fast, loves the sun, and is semi-evergreen. Waxy yellow saucer-shaped blooms appear in profusion from late spring right though to autumn.

• *Garrya elliptica* is a shade-loving evergreen that bears extraordinary flower tassels on the male plants in winter.

• *Pyracantha* is a thorny evergreen that looks superb when trained very formally. Hawthorn-like flowers in early summer lead to masses of yellow, orange or red berries in autumn and winter.

52 are you sitting comfortably?

Whether you're by yourself, with a lover or in company, whether you're nodding off, keeping an eye on children or watching pets play, you will always need a little something for the family seat. From classic wooden benches by revered architect Sir Edwin Lutyens to cutting-edge ball chairs by designer Finn Stone, there's a whole host of fabulous furniture out there. Why on earth settle for second best?

shake your booty
Never buy seating without trying it out. That rules out mail-order and internet 'bargains' straightaway.

a pain in the proverbial
A seat should suit your hips and thighs, the backrest should acknowledge the curvature of your spine. You're in for years of grief if they don't.

a bum steer
Wriggle! Some chairs and benches are so insubstantial that they creak and sway under the weight of their occupants. Look for solid support and legs that are securely braced.

cheek to cheek
A two-seater that can't accommodate two people with plenty of room to spare might as well be a chair. A three-seater should be very amply proportioned indeed or it will only ever be used as a two seater.

lounging around 53

Nothing is more opulent than a reclining chair or a sun-lounger. They take up loads of space of course, but they're great for large gardens, and in small spaces they're perfect for hard-working young couples and for parents whose children have flown the nest.

• Wooden loungers can stay out in all kinds of weather. Some are so ergonomically designed that they are blissfully comfortable just as they are. No need for any cushions!

• Conservatory loungers can take a holiday in the garden when the weather is fine – along with plenty of cushions and throws you can really snuggle down into.

• Streamlined modern loungers are available with steel or aluminium frames covered in fabric as resilient as the sails on yachts. Make a splash!

• Got two sturdy trees close by? Sling up a hammock! Zzzzzzzzz . . . .

• For something more pukka, get a colonial swing seat complete with awning.

pull up a chair 54

Whether we're gossiping or eating we've never had it so good so far as flexible, easily moved seating is concerned. With rattan look-alike armchairs that are impervious to rain and frost, wrought-iron dining chairs galvanised against rust, and sheer plastic carvers that let the garden shine through in all its glory, we're spoilt for choice. Don't simply regard chairs as practical pieces of furniture, look on them as works of art and invest in the best you can possibly afford.

plastic, acrylic and fibreglass

- Easy to wipe clean or hose down
- Come in a wide range of colours
- Lightweight, waterproof and frost-proof

iron

- Very, very strong, but heavy to lift
- Mostly suited to traditional settings
- Can be cold to sit on

tubular steel and aluminium

- Lightweight, weatherproof and strong
- Adventurous modern styling
- Come in satin and polished finishes

wood

- Looks natural, is natural, suits any garden
- Quality hardwoods mellow to silver with age
- Timber doesn't always come from sustainable forestry

stowaway seating

55

Some gardens are so small that the area you can sacrifice to permanent seating is severely limited. Thankfully, it's not only deckchairs that fold away. Pavilion-style chairs in wrought iron and wood, even whole benches can be collapsed flat. If you can find sturdy enough hooks, this type of furniture looks great hanging on an external wall when not in use.

Alternatively, find chairs that stack. Some craftsman-built wooden chairs sit beautifully on top of each other, though you'd never guess by looking at them.

Indoor/outdoor seating is arguably the most accommodating option: Philippe Starck's designs are known around the world; seats woven from man-made Hularo closely resemble those made from split cane.

garden tables

Where would any garden be without a lovely table?

small is beautiful

At a café type table you can read the papers, enjoy a glass of wine or take a light informal meal.

material choice

The material you choose can reflect the style of your garden. For example, wooden slats look great with decking, wirework sits prettily amongst country cottage plantings, and steel mesh suits the idiom of inner-city balconies and roof gardens.

solid or permeable

'Holey' surfaces let rainwater through and dry off quickly but they are devils where cutlery, pens and tall glasses are concerned. Solid plastic, wood or slate tables often need wiping down before use, but on the plus side they offer greater stability.

desks and things

Outdoor dining tables are of course perfect for serious entertaining, but they have many more uses besides. Use yours as a potting bench or an outdoor desk.

clean-up time

Don't be a party pooper. Give your table a really good scrub at the end of winter and watch out all year round for insanitary contributions from wildlife.

hold that cloth

For a really special occasion you might like to use a tablecloth – go for cool crisp linen if you can – but an old sheet can do sterling service if you need to hem a hole in the middle to take a parasol. Either buy workaday drawing-board clips from a stationer's to hold it in place or look out for decorative tablecloth clips in the shape of flowers, leaves, pebbles or butterflies.

the hole experience

When buying a large table always ensure that there's a hole in the middle to take the shaft of a sunshade. It's a nuisance – sometimes even downright impossible – to add one later on. It's useful to offer shade for outdoor lunch parties, and it's essential if you are working outdoors on your laptop.

on show

Some tables are purely for display: low stone tables in particular are perfect for displaying shallow bowls of alpines and succulents.

artistic ambition

Never mind all their practical applications, tables can be attractive additions to your garden in their own right. They are wonderful vehicles for mosaic or for colourful hand-painted tiles.

indoors out

On a fine summer's evening why not be really decadent and carry your indoor dining suite outdoors?

56

10 ideas

cool shades 57

We have all been warned by the experts of how prolonged exposure to scorching sun can lead to irreparable skin damage. Children, blondes and baldies are most at risk but everyone should take care, which is why it pays to have some shade in the garden. The options that you can buy range from parasols that stick in the grass or fix into a weighted base, to traditional fold-down stripy awnings and modern tensile canopies suspended on wires.

parasols

Some loungers and deckchairs come equipped with detachable shades that help protect your face. Some freestanding parasols have stems that can be kinked in the middle to angle them against the sun; others have cantilevered supports and can hang right over you. Parasols come in Japanese waxed paper with bamboo struts, in oiled canvas and sturdy teak, or in man-made fibres on lightweight metal frames.

- Translucent waxed-paper parasols might look elegant, but they have to be put under cover every evening and whipped inside at the first hint of rain.
- Canvas is tough and durable, but is susceptible to damp stains and mildew in winter.
- Man-made fibres are far and away the most weather-resistant, but all too often they come in strident colours. Choose cream or earth tones if possible.

awning, yawning

Though they are useful and easily folded away, the limiting factor with conventional awnings is that they have to be attached to a wall – and that's not always where you need the shade.

summer lovin'

Modern tensile canopies look great strung across courtyard gardens. Besides protecting you from glare, they afford a great deal of privacy from neighbours.

green canopies 58

The softly dappled light beneath a beautiful tree is arguably the most enchanting form of shade but few of us have such a tree. However, it is relatively quick and easy to install a pergola, archway or gazebo that can be cloaked in climbers for shade.

pergolas

- Pillared walkways with top beams have been garden features for centuries. They can be of brick, stone, cast iron, or timber, and should stand at least 2.5m high to allow dangling space for flowers above people's heads.
- Consider an arcade running along the side of your house or against a boundary wall.
- An alleyway of green hazel boughs bent into shape is an attractive but short-term alternative.

archways

A well-proportioned archway can be a generous source of shade.

Against a wall it becomes an arbour – the perfect place to put a bench.

gazebos

Freestanding, open pavilions for admiring the view were eighteenth-century garden favourites. Buy yours ready-made in wirework, assemble a tubular steel kit, or build a timber one.

classic plants for pergolas

There are many climbers to choose from, just avoid anything that has thorns.

clematis

Plant a mixture of early, mid-season and late-flowering varieties for a really splendid show. Lightly prune 'earlies' immediately after flowering, give 'mids' a general tidy in early spring and cut 'lates' to within 20cm of the ground.

grape

Vitis vinifera is a beautiful specimen. Fresh spring-time foliage is joined by dangling clusters of fruit that ripen late in summer. Autumn leaf colour can be spectacular.

potato vine

The star-like white or lilac-to-purple flowers of the semi-evergreen *Solanum crispum* are far prettier than the common name might suggest.

sweet pea

Lathyrus odoratus, the annual sweet pea bears its beautiful blooms in late summer to early autumn with a deliciously sweet fragrance. Named cultivars are legion.

wisteria

Of the ten or so species, Chinese wisteria, *W. sinensis* and Japanese wisteria, *W. floribunda* are the most commonly grown. Purple or white blooms appear early in summer, but bear in mind that the flower clusters of Japanese varieties can be up to 60cm long, so build high and mind your head!

59

let there be light

Lighting not only adds hours to the enjoyment we get from our gardens, it opens up a whole range of dazzling effects. What's more, it makes outdoor spaces safer and our homes more secure. All thanks to the flick of a switch, the action of a timer, or the trigger of a dusk or movement sensor.

live!

Electricity can be dangerous. Match or exceed local building regulations with regard to protective sheathing on cables and circuit breakers that cut off the power should water get to the wiring. Low-voltage systems fed through a transformer are generally cheaper and safer to install than those that are connected directly to the mains supply.

earth . . .

Garden cabling that is buried rather than wall-mounted requires a depth far beyond the ordinary reach of spade or fork. Before filling in your excavation make a detailed plan of where the cables lie and either put a thick layer of sand on top or else a brightly striped plastic tape so that future residents won't unwittingly dig too deep.

solar power

Solar garden lights are entirely self-contained. You can site them wherever you like and as long as they get enough sun by day, they'll switch themselves on for several hours each night. They can be great fun in summertime, especially those that slowly range through all the colours of the spectrum. Don't rely on them for serious task lighting though. On dark winter evenings, when you really need them, their reserves are at their lowest.

task lighting

Use lights to make your garden practical and safe at night. Don't fumble around in the dark!

paths and driveways

Guiding lights are both welcoming and reassuring at night. Outline main routes using paired low-level lanterns or recessed uplighters.

steps

Safety really matters here. Recess sturdy little spots in the treads, run thin neon strips under overhanging treads, or wall-mount lights beside the treads. If none of these are practicable, install a diffuse overhead light source such as a lantern on a pillar.

doorways

You want to find your keyhole easily when you're returning home late. It's also good to know who's calling when you peer through your peephole from inside. Visitors need to see the number of your house and to be able to find your doorbell or knocker. A pair of lamps either side of the front door will flatter your home, cast no awkward shadows, and light up the faces of your guests.

water

Ponds reflect light beautifully by night, and a few wide beams skimming the surface will prevent any accidents. If your pool is crystal clear use underwater lighting.

security

No intruder wants to be seen on the prowl, so install a movement sensor. If anything suspicious goes on outdoors after lights-out your whole system will turn on in a flash.

61 decorative lights

Some lights are employed not only as sources of illumination but also as decorative elements in their own right. Some dissolve into their surroundings by day. Others make a statement 24/7.

fairy lights

Strings of tiny bulbs are incredibly pretty. Plain or coloured, still or twinkling they look spellbinding wound around the branches of trees and large shrubs. Make sure not to buy the kind where one loose or faulty bulb knocks out the whole system. Ask your retailer for advice.

fibre optics

Fibre-optic cables carry light from a powerful remote source to the tips of tiny filaments. Set them into concrete floors and rendered walls to shimmer like distant stars; use them to bring life to waterfalls and fountains; add a post-modern touch by letting them spill about just as they are.

lanterns

Where to begin? There are reproduction carriage lamps, wall lights like those on the bulkheads of ships, or sleek modern fittings that look as though they've leapt from the pages of some wildly smart interiors magazine. Oriental lanterns sway on the ends of crooked sticks, luminous pillars pulse in all kinds of colours. Illuminated bollards in concrete, brushed steel, rusted iron and even teak vie for our attention. The best advice? Choose whatever lantern sits best with the style of your garden.

special effects

These professional techniques are all about drama. The harder it is to identify the light source the better.

spotlighting

Spotlights on a stage draw attention to the stars of the show. Bright, tightly focussed beams shining on the odd sculpture, bench or tree add drama to your garden. Don't overdo it though – too large a cast and you've got an amateur musical on your hands.

grazing

A wide-angled, diffuse light running straight up or straight down any vertical surface reveals both texture and architectural detail. Grazing introduces contrast to the evening garden: walls, fences and hedges acquire a fascinating glow, but their immediate surroundings stay in the dark.

uplighting

Soft but strong lights, especially coloured ones, shining up tree trunks and into their branches are an absolutely enchanting feature.

moonlighting

Pale white light filtering down through a canopy of leaves gives an illusion of moonlight. Magical.

backlighting

Lighting something from behind creates a bold black silhouette. Bamboos and grasses acquire a whole new dimension and bold foliage plants with clean-cut outlines look stunning. One well-placed fixture can graze a wall and backlight a plant – so much more interesting than shining a spotlight on them both.

projection

A recent innovation derived from theatres and nightclubs, projectors cast colours and patterns onto garden walls or floors. You can project figurative artworks and abstracts alike, present a sequence of slides, and suggest moving clouds or rippling water.

63 an old flame

candles

A garden illuminated by candles is seductive and mysterious. They are a quick and simple way of beautifully dressing your garden for a special occasion: the glow is warm, mellow and immensely flattering; the flickering flames have life and vitality. Candles are neither cost-effective nor the least bit practical for long-term use, but they do give a lovely light.

Dumpy little candles that can't topple over are perfect for instant outdoor lighting. Tea lights, night lights – call them what you will – can be dotted round just as they are, or better still, can be put into a whole range of containers – jewel-coloured, gilded Moroccan tea glasses, purpose-made glass lanterns in oriental, antique or contemporary styles, simple domestic jam jars hung by wire from trees.

Floating candles for shallow bowls of water come in pretty shapes and colours. Put some pebbles at the bottom of the water for added interest, scatter a few flowerheads or petals on the surface then place the whole arrangement either on the ground or on a low table where it can be seen in all its glory.

Tall, elegant candles can be a problem: they need to be really secure, and they are prone to being blown out by the wind. Use candlesticks and candelabra only where you can really appreciate them and attend to them – on your outdoor dining table. Elsewhere, you'll need glazed or perforated metal lanterns to hold them tight.

Large fat candles that come in their own pots are now commonplace. They have thick, reliable wicks and many are scented – either to heighten the romantic atmosphere or, more prosaically, to keep insects at bay. As with all candles, light them just before it gets dark.

torches

Oil lamps are the oldest lighting known to man. Contemporary designs for the garden include neat conical glass flares that can be spiked into lawns, burners carved in stone, and zinc flambeaux on sturdy bamboo poles.

gel burners

Ignite a pot of flammable gel and you've got a really dramatic light. The floor, tabletop and wall-mounted fittings you can buy are fine, but remember that there are no standard sizes so you might find yourself tied into a particular refill. Then again, you might like to make a holder of your own by pouring pebbles round a pot of gel in a wide-mouthed flowerpot or a small tin bucket.

five flame precautions

1 • Don't put living flames close to anything that could catch light.

2 • Never leave young children or pets unsupervised near flames.

3 • Pinch, blow or snuff out every candle or torch flame after use.

4 • To put out a gel burner you need to starve it of oxygen with a close-fitting lid. Make sure you've got something suitable to hand.

5 • Consider buying a small dry powder or foam fire extinguisher – just in case. Or get a fire blanket. You want to light your garden, not torch your home.

turn up the heat

64

The sun is our primary source of natural outdoor heat. It only
has to be hidden by clouds for a few moments for us to feel
the difference. All other things being equal, a shady garden
will be cooler than a light and bright one.

Something else comes into play though: the breeze. Wind-
chill factors aren't just technical asides in winter weather
forecasts; they're a fact of everyday life, and they bring the
temperature down. Think, for example, of sunbathing on a
hot and sunny beach first with and then without a fabric
windbreak. That is why you'll tend to feel warmer sitting
outside in a sheltered courtyard than perched on an exposed
roof terrace.

When you're moving around working in the garden your
muscles generate heat and you rarely notice the cold. But it's
a different story when you're relaxing, so put chairs and
tables in the sunniest, most sheltered corner of your garden.
Buildings reflect an awful lot of heat so the closer you are to
a sunny wall the warmer you'll be. Homes with central
heating also radiate warmth through windows and doors –
something worth bearing in mind on fine days in late spring
and early autumn.

Having made the most of what you've got by day, there 's
plenty more you can do to raise the temperature at night.
Install an outdoor heater (see 65). Get a hot tub (see 68).
Whatever lights your fire.

hot stuff

Outdoor heaters range from the practical but stylish to the positively primeval. Take your pick from these offerings and bask in the warmth.

gas heaters

Umbrella heaters using canisters of liquid propane or butane as fuel are far and away the safest form of outdoor heating. They keep you toasty warm, the temperature is adjustable, and they're quick and easy to turn on and off. With one of these on permanent standby you'll find yourself lunching, dining, chatting and canoodling outdoors far more often than you'd ever have thought possible.

Wall-mounted gas heaters are also available; these are great for really small gardens and narrow balconies.

chimeneas

These solid-fuel heaters have their origins in Mexico where the pot-bellied stove and chimney were formed out of mud or river clay. They are now produced in terracotta, but only the highest quality versions survive the wet and frost of cooler climates, so choose your chimenea wisely. Once the coal, wood or charcoal gets going it will throw out a vast amount of heat for a long period of time.

fire pits

A sunken hearth can be magical. Build one in brick or better still have a metalworker craft one in stainless steel. The secret to keeping the fire alive is oxygen, so use a generous grate and run a thin metal pipe from the base of the pit to an out-of-the-way place above ground. The flames will draw fresh air in through this flue.

braziers

Metal baskets for burning logs or coals look spectacular. Really stylish ones look good even when they're empty, but why not use your empty one as a cache pot to hide an easily removed container full of plants?

bonfires

If you want to give a man a treat let him build a bonfire. It's guaranteed to bring out his primitive hunter-gatherer instincts. Don't expect much heat, though; he won't let you stand anywhere near it.

5 ideas

barbecue 66

We all know that a barbecue is a boy's second favourite toy.

- Barbecues can be built into retaining walls to give you storage space beneath.
- You can buy fabulous Japanese-style tiled barbecues that double as ovens.
- Some come gas-fired in stainless steel and use volcanic ash in lieu of charcoal.
- Far-eastern terracotta barbecues work both as open grills and tandoori ovens.
- Petrol stations, garden centres and supermarkets sell throwaway ones at giveaway prices.

Choose a barbecue that fits comfortably into your price range and that will give you optimum utility. If you entertain infrequently then a rusty old pile of rubbish in a corner is not only a waste of space but an eyesore. You're better off buying the occasional disposable barbecue. If you often have friends round then give pride of place to something really state-of-the-art that you can fire up in an instant.

safety first
- Never put a barbecue under a tree or within scorching distance of plants.
- Site it where prevailing winds blow the smoke away from your home.
- Don't use starter fluid. Do you want to poison your guests?
- Most important of all, invite your neighbours round to join you.

67

don't forget the food

Meat of all kinds, oily fish, and fleshy vegetables like peppers, sliced aubergines and corn-on-the-cob taste delicious when grilled over glowing embers. They are especially good when they have been marinated beforehand: aromatic baths of oils, herbs and spices not only tenderise meat, they fill it with flavour and keep it from drying out as it cooks.

Buy tender meat like steak, young lamb and chicken breasts. If you haven't got an outdoor dining table then choose finger-friendly food like chops, drumsticks and home-made kebabs.

five practical pointers

1 • Flames quickly scorch the food outside and leave it raw inside. Only begin grilling when the fire has died down and the red-hot coals are covered in grey ash.

2 • Adjust the heat by raising or lowering the grill.

3 • Soak wooden skewers in water overnight to keep the ends from charring or burning.

4 • Oil the grill to keep food from sticking.

5 • Cooking times are unpredictable, so have bowls of crudités and olives to hand for guests to nibble on without spoiling their appetite. And make sure there's plenty to drink.

accompaniments

A selection of salads, some good bread for mopping up all the juices, and perhaps a little fresh fruit for afters are all you need to complete a truly memorable outdoor meal.

68 soak the blues away

What could be more luxurious than a hot tub? Whether it's an intimate wooden barrel for two or a large sunken pool in cast acrylic for sharing with friends, a tub of steaming, swirling water is the height of outdoor decadence. (But as with gigolos, mistresses and yachts, if you have to ask the price you can't afford one.) Aim for comfortable integrated seating, an insulated hull that minimises heat loss, and a sturdy and secure cover to protect the water and to prevent children from climbing in unsupervised.

Debris must be filtered away before reaching the pumping system, and scrupulous standards of hygiene must be maintained at all times. You need to empty collection traps regularly, and replace filter cartridges in accordance with the manufacturer's instructions. The idea is to relax in crystal-clear water, not stew in primordial soup.

Hydrotherapy jets are a must. They massage away stress and banish fatigue. They are also great fun. Tubs for serious party animals include coloured lighting and stereos. Give one a whirl!

69 make a splash

Water is an integral part of the natural landscape and a versatile element that deserves a place in every garden.

time for reflection

Deep dark pools reflect the shapes and colours of their surroundings. They do this with mirror-like accuracy when they are calm and still, in muted shades on overcast days, and with ripples and distortions when the surface is disturbed by wind or rain.

permanent residents

Water can play permanent host to goldfish and to beautiful aquatic plants.

occasional visitors

Ponds are valuable resources for passing wildlife. Shallow margins allow birds to bathe and they make it easy for amphibians to clamber in and out between meals of slugs and snails.

10 ideas

rainwater special

A whole new habitat! Harness rainwater run-off with a pierced plastic liner to create an area specially suited to bog plants like candelabra primulas.

rest your legs

Generous coping stones atop the walls of raised ponds can provide attractive and functional seating.

falling water

Consider installing a fountain in a formal pool or, in a naturalistic setting, building a waterfall. Water constantly on the move never fails to catch the eye – it sparkles in the sunshine and catches the lamplight by night.

sounds divine

The gentle murmur of a bubble fountain is music to the ears, and a hidden sump allows you to adapt and develop the theme visually.

space miser

Where space is at a premium, install a self-contained wall water feature with an endlessly trickling spout.

go with the flow

Flowing rills of barely any depth lend dynamism to level surfaces like patios or create miniature cascades down the sides of steps.

stay safe

Water can ripple over a stainless-steel sculpture, run down a wall of glass, or shoot through the air before draining magically away. Such approaches to water design are the safest where children are concerned.

70

ponder this

Large brass bowls, horse troughs, stoneware sinks and cast-iron animal feeders can be given a whole new lease of life as miniature garden pools. But if you've got more space, then why not go for the full works?

preformed

First consider a preformed pond liner. The ground must be levelled then excavated to match its contours. Dig a little deeper and wider than strictly necessary then line the hole with a generous layer of wet sand to act as a buffer between the liner and any sharp stones.

freeform

Sheets of PVC, or better still of longer-lasting butyl, give more design flexibility. After planning or marking out your pool, you'll need to buy a sheet that is as long as the pool plus twice its maximum depth and as wide as the pool plus twice its maximum depth. Centre it over your sand-lined hollow then allow it to sink into shape by slowly filling the pool with a hosepipe. Disguise the edge with bricks, slabs or pebbles (which you can concrete into position) then trim off any excess.

formal

The grandest, most expensive pools are those raised in brick or stone. They should be sealed with a custom-made welded rubber liner, and their walls must be very strong indeed.

A cheaper alternative for a square or circular pool is an excavation lined in concrete. Angle the sides at 20 degrees or so to the vertical then line it with chicken wire for strength. Trowel on a stiff mix of concrete to a thickness of around 15cm. Concrete for ponds is usually darkened with dye, and you should make sure that it incorporates water- and frost-proofing additives.

pond life

Still water left barren and untended quickly turns green, slimy and smelly. Introduce plants and fish though and it will more or less look after itself.

instant ecosystem

A healthy pool is a crystal-clear ecosystem: fish graze on algae and help control mosquito larvae and other aquatic insects; plants absorb carbon dioxide respired by fish, feed on their waste and supply animal life with oxygen; insects, molluscs and lower life-forms scavenge and mop up the products of decomposition. Introduce a little bit of everything straightaway.

submerged aquatics

Simply take an assortment of hardy submerged pondweeds like *Ceratophyllum demersum*, *Elodea canadensis*, *Lagarosiphon major* and *Myriophyllum aquaticum* and plop them into the water at a rate of approximately five bunches per surface square metre. Fast growing, you'll need to keep them under control by lifting out any surplus with a net.

floating plants

Again, no planting required – *Eichornia crassipes*, *Pistia stratiotes* and *Stratiotes aloides* just float on the water and spread quickly to provide a carpet of greenery that keeps algae under control and provides welcome shade for fish. You should aim to cover between half and three-quarters of the pond surface with foliage by the height of summer.

water lilies

Miniature water lilies can thrive in containers with barely 15cm of water above their crowns but the really vigorous cultivars require as much as 50cm and are better suited to lakes. Good *Nymphaea* varieties for domestic ponds include the dwarf yellow-flowered *N.* 'Pygmaea Helvola', the small white scented *N. odorata* var. *minor*, and the medium-sized double pink *N.* 'Madame Wilfron Gonnère'.

marginals

Grow these in damp soil in very shallow water at the edge of a pool to add colour, height and form. *Iris ensata* 'Rose Queen' is a breathtaking clematis-flowered iris of Japan; low-growing *Houttuynia cordata variegata* has green, yellow, orange and red heart-shaped leaves that smell of tangerines when crushed; *Schoenoplectus lacustris* subsp. *tabernaemontani* 'Zebrinus' is a tongue-twisting eye-catching rush with leaves like porcupine quills banded cream and green.

planting

Some preformed ponds have built-in planting pockets as opposed to simple shelves for containers. Don't buy them. 'Breathable' open mesh black plastic pots are best as they allow you to move plants around at will and lift them easily for division. Line pots with sacking to prevent soil escaping, use special aquatic compost that is low in nutrients, and put a thick layer of gravel on top to prevent fish from muddying the water. Should you buy water lilies already in growth, lower the pots gradually to their optimum depth as the stems of the leaves lengthen, either by moving them down a shelf or two, or by perching them in the middle of the pool on a pile of bricks that you slowly reduce in height.

ornamental fish

Introduce the fish after about a month. Simplest is to buy variations on the common goldfish, *Carassius auratus auratus* – all of which grow in proportion to the size of their pool. Get them from a reputable supplier. In a well-established pool there should be enough natural food to keep them happy, but if you want to fatten them up on flakes, sticks or other proprietary treats, give them only as much as they can scoff in five minutes – otherwise the leftovers will sink to the bottom and rot.

Koi require specially filtered water and destroy all the plants in sight. Catfish

attack, maim and even eat other species. Never release garden pondlife into the wild.

wildlife

A large number of microscopic species arrive along with the plants you buy. For the rest, consider introducing some ramshorn snails, *Planorbis corneus*, to keep down thread algae, and some swan mussels, *Anodonta cygnea* or painters' mussels, *Unio pictorum*. Frogs, toads, lizards and the like will find their own way in just so long as your pool has shallow sides, some stepping stones or a pebble beach for easy access.

perimeter plantings

If there's a permanently damp overspill at one side or another of your pool you can extend your range of moisture-loving plants. Be careful though not to 'fence' your pond in. The idea is to enhance its beauty, not obscure it.

maintenance

Get the balance right and you won't need to do anything besides clearing away dying foliage in autumn. If a pond is too green it needs more floating plants for shade. If it's full of dirty brown sediment you're probably overfeeding your fish.

10
ideas

keep it moving

Whether you're looking at a spouting lion's head, at water bubbling over a millstone to trickle softly through gravel, or at a copper tree dripping rain from its leaves, the principle behind all re-circulating features is the same: a submerged pump sends the water off to do its stuff then gravity brings it home again, ad infinitum. Having grasped the basic concept, you can really play around.

• Try putting a pump in the bottom of a waterproof glazed pot against a wall and extending its spout to just below the rim. Almost fill the pot with pebbles, and hide the electric cable under a couple of overlapping stones where it runs over the back edge. Top the whole thing up with water, turn on the pump then tinker with the pebbles to get the bubble effect you're after.

• The most basic sump is an underground tank topped with a sturdy metal grille that can be covered with pebbles. Some look like upturned sombreros, these are the most efficient as the rim helps catch splashes that would otherwise be lost to the system. Run a flexible pipe from the submerged pump to make a ribbed Greek oil jar overflow forever, to make a watering can pour indefinitely, to run a Japanese bamboo deer-scarer, to do anything you please. Effects can easily be combined: a wall spout, for example, can fill a trough to overflowing before the water goes to ground.

where weight's an issue

You can't excavate a balcony or roof terrace to make a pool, and weight issues will often rule out water-filled vessels of any decent size, so how can you have a water feature there? Purpose-made wall features are ideal for balconies while freestanding water sculptures are the best option for roofs. Because these only hold a small amount of water they need frequent top-ups to replace what is lost through evaporation.

73

jet set

What could be more dynamic or thrilling than a fountain? Jets of water can whoosh straight upwards to come tumbling down all around in a flurry of white. They can be aimed through the air in parabolic arcs. High-pressure lamina jets can even shoot slugs of water like bullets from a gun.

with a pond . . .

Fountains for ponds look and sound best with a fine, light spray. For practical reasons the smaller the expanse of water, the lower you have to make the jet – otherwise wind will habitually blow the water wide of the mark and your pond will slowly empty.

. . . or without

You don't need a pond to have a fountain or two. All the wirework and plumbing can be concealed beneath innocent-looking paving or brickwork. When the power is on, the jets come straight from the ground and the water drains direct back to the sump. Children adore this kind of thing, especially when the fountains play in sequence: they dare themselves to run through. Make sure there are always some surprises in store. No unpleasant ones though – you should use purifying tablets to keep the system clean.

contain your excitement

74

Growing plants in containers is a satisfying and flexible approach to gardening. In a small yard, a balcony or a roof terrace, containers of one kind or another are the only way of introducing flowers and foliage. Pots are also the perfect finishing touch for larger gardens.

virtue of necessity

Containers full of plants aren't only beautiful, they are practical, too. Wall-mounted in small spaces they give you greenery with no loss of floor space. They can disguise manhole covers and mask outdoor gas and electricity meters. If you live in rented accommodation or if you move home often, they're a great way to invest in a garden all of your own.

looking good

Containers should be decorative objects in their own right, and the best-looking examples can even be left empty!

a fresh perspective

Soldierly rows of containers draw the eye and lend a strong sense of perspective, especially if they are planted up identically. In general though, bold clusters of pots make more of an impact: they are easier to maintain and create a warm and sheltered microclimate for plants to thrive in.

composition tricks

Arranging and rearranging a group of containers is an excellent way of learning about composition. Begin with the large and the tall, then work forward to the small and the shallow. Any container that is especially appealing should either have something very low in front of it or be placed in full view at the side.

centre of attention

Foregrounding an attractive pot or two is the container-garden equivalent of featuring large specimen plants towards the front of a border: it changes the rhythm and catches the eye. Making really good pieces the centre of attention gives the impression that everything else is pretty darn fine too, and you can then get away with cheap black plastic pots in the deep dark background.

change and change about

Besides rearranging existing displays you can constantly add new pots and replant old ones. Whether you want a different look for each season using short-lived bedding plants, an ever-growing permanent collection or a combination of the two, containers make it easy.

little green fingers

Fast, finite results encourage children of all sizes to get in on the act. They'll quickly become gardeners in their own right if you give them carte blanche to plant up a container or two with their own choice.

the right stuff

Soil-based composts are ideal for most situations, but lightweight peat- or coir- based ones sometimes make more sense on balconies and roof terraces. Plants with special needs are easily accommodated: use free-draining gritty compost for succulents, and ericaceous compost for lime-hating plants like azaleas, camellias and heathers. Good quality composts have about six-months' worth of nutrients in them.

good drainage

Keep the compost in containers from getting sodden, turning sour, and causing your plant roots to rot by having adequate drainage. Ensure that all containers have holes at the bottom. Cover these with a generous layer of small pebbles, broken slates or terracotta crocks to keep the soil in while letting surplus water out. Soil-based composts are the easiest to water and are the most free-draining. Others are hard to re-wet when they dry out in summer and they often turn into claggy peat bogs over winter.

effective watering

Frequent trickles rarely do more than moisten the surface, so give containers a really good drenching once in a while. Good news: you can't over-water a well-drained pot. Bad news: the water that trickles away leaches nutrients from the compost. Solution? Buy some fertiliser.

window boxes

The optimum size for a window box is as deep as your sill and as wide as the window. To maximise the light that gets into your home, consider wall-mounting the box somewhat below the level of the sill. This also makes your windows seem taller and more elegant. And above ground-floor level it's wise insurance to hook, wire or tie each window box so you don't have any accidents.

materials

Terracotta is less inclined than plastic or fibreglass to fly off in a breeze and it helps insulate roots against extremes of temperature – and if it's glazed, the soil inside won't dry out as quickly. Lead window boxes are fantastically expensive, but they look superb against older style properties. If you can't find the size or style you're after, consider custom-made planters in wood.

insulation extra

Thin-walled containers, especially those in zinc-galvanised steel, can freeze roots in winter and bake them in summer. Insulate them against frost and scorching sunshine by lining them with several layers of newspaper before putting in the compost.

splashing around

When you plant up a window box – or indeed any container – leave a couple of centimetres between the top of the compost and the rim of the pot to make watering easier. To prevent soil ricocheting onto the window in pelting rain, scatter a thick mulch of gravel over the surface.

Really dashing window boxes use a combination of plants that stand upright and plants that hang down.

uppers

Ornamental cabbages and capsicums, heathers and cyclamen give you colour from early autumn right through winter. Spring bulbs fill the gap before summertime, at which point you're really spoilt for choice. Twiggy or contorted sticks poked in amongst tall-growing flowers like narcissus or lilies not only lend support, they have great visual appeal. Dwarf conifers and evergreen euonymus provide backbone all year round.

downers

Ivy is the obvious foliage plant for trailing down the front of window boxes, but consider helichrysum, plectranthus, spider plants and ground ivy (*Glechoma hederacea*), too. Flowers that trail beautifully include aubretia, bidens, mesembryanthemums, nasturtiums, ivy-leaved pelargoniums, the golden form of Creeping Jenny (*Lysimachia nummularia*), and the exotic parrot's beak (*Lotus berthelotii*).

76 hanging baskets, balls and swags

Flanking a doorway, decorating a pergola or running the length of a wall, baskets, balls and swags are a knockout.

step by step

1 • To hold in as much moisture as possible use a really spongy peat- or coir-based compost and mix in granules of water-retaining gel.

2 • The smaller your plants when you buy them the better. Plugs in polystyrene trays are ideal. You can afford to use them generously and their capacity for growth is phenomenal. If the gaps in your wire mesh aren't as wide as you'd like, wrap their roots in stiff paper to push them into position.

3 • When planting a basket work from the bottom to the top. Poke young plants through the holes then line the mesh with sphagnum moss and back-fill with compost as you go.

4 • Plants generally grow quickly and thirstily so summer hanging baskets need a really thorough watering at least once a day and a decent feed once a week.

5 • Use strong brackets and chains to support your hanging baskets. They might feel pretty light when they're first planted up, but once they're watered and growth is underway, they'll get heavier day by day. For safety and security's sake, wire the chains into place so your pride and joy can't be blown down or carried off in the night.

make a break with tradition

For something really spectacular wire two hanging baskets together to form a solid globe. Planted with mat-forming succulents like sempervivums it will look fantastic in a modern, streamlined setting. These balls also make interesting accent pieces either empty or with potted plants trapped inside.

Plastic pouches for walls and fences – a little like vertical growing bags – are now widely available. They also come as long swags that hang in festoons. They are an excellent way of decorating boundaries in the summer months.

ten basket cases

1 • *Begonia*   Stick to small-flowered varieties
2 • *Brachyscome iberidifolia*   Swan River daisies tolerate a fair degree of drought
3 • *Campanula isophylla*   This bellflower comes in white, blue and violet
4 • *Impatiens walleriana*   Busy Lizzies are a sensible choice for shade
5 • *Fuchsia*   Great blooms in late summer and early autumn
6 • *Isotoma axillaris*   The flowers are fragrant in the evening and after rainfall
7 • *Lobelia erinus*   Not only blue but also white, pink, red and lilac
8 • *Lobularia maritima*   Sweet alyssum has a creamy froth of honey-scented flowers
9 • *Pelargonium*   Varieties with coloured leaves have double the impact
10 • *Petunia*   The Surfinia Series is especially vigorous

something old(ish)

Gardeners through the centuries have grown plants in a wide variety of containers, so there's a vast heritage to draw on: elaborately carved stone urns and vases; lead planters from the eighteenth century; cast-iron gems from the Industrial Revolution; hand-thrown terracotta ranging from artisan flowerpots to Arts and Crafts masterpieces.

repro

Garden antiques suffer the ravages of time and the elements much more than indoor pieces, so genuine articles are in short supply and prices are high. That is why more and more manufacturers are making quality reproductions. Cast stone pieces cost a fraction of the pieces they are modelled after.

Independent potteries are reviving the techniques of past generations. The processes used by foundries haven't changed in centuries. A good reproduction may be an antique of tomorrow.

fake!

• Distress brand-spanking new cast stone with a hammer and chisel then smear dirt and yoghurt into the wounds to give mosses and lichens a toe-hold.
• White paint, heavily thinned and lightly daubed, gives a chalky, mineral-encrusted look to terracotta.
• Lead quickly patinates of its own accord. Iron soon rusts, but an alternative is to give it several coats of slightly different coloured paint that can then be artfully bashed, sanded and flaked away.

something new

Modern containers come in all forms and materials.

clay

The best contemporary ceramics are never to be found in the shops. Artist potters usually sell direct from their studios or through exhibitions at craft fairs and flower shows.

concrete

Concrete can be reinforced with glass fibres and made almost as thin as bone china. It can be pigmented with natural minerals or with vibrant chemical dyes. It can be cast in high relief, or be made very thick indeed to be deeply embossed. Large concrete pieces are generally cast to order, so you can often specify precisely the colour and finish you require.

metals

Spun or cast aluminium vessels are now widely available, so are double-skinned planters that appear to be solid and heavy yet are light as a feather. Metals work brilliantly in modern urban settings.

plastics and fibreglass

Words once pronounced with a sneer are now close to poetry. These synthetic materials are lightweight, self-coloured and durable. They can be moulded into fantastic forms and because they lend themselves to mass-production, they come cheap. They can also be made to imitate other materials. They're the future!

79 something borrowed

Improvised containers show that you've got style and imagination. Many come absolutely free, others at knock-down prices. Develop a theme or take an eclectic approach. They've got little or no intrinsic value so you can afford to play around, and never mind that some will last only a few seasons; simply keep an eye out for replacements.

baskets

Whether woven from willow, hazel or rattan, basketware is perfect for the garden. Shopping bags, hampers, laundry baskets and storage trays are designed to hold all sorts of clobber, so why not plants? Tightly woven containers can take compost just as they are. Others will need lining with plastic – black bin bags are fine. Just be sure to pierce them all over for drainage and soil aeration.

bath tubs

Cast-iron roll top baths are beautiful objects, so even if they're damaged it seems wicked to consign them to the scrapyard. Give them a new lease of life in the garden by filling them with shrubs and large perennials, leaving room at the edges for container plants that can overflow the sides in a graceful manner.

boats

Dinghies and rowing boats that are no longer ship-shape look great in seaside or riverside gardens. They look good part-submerged at a jaunty angle, barely half-filled with soil, and with a loose, naturalistic feel. Give the impression that the boat has finally washed up and that flowers and foliage are slowly taking command. As with a bath tub, you must give serious consideration to the precise site. Once it's full of compost it will be going nowhere fast.

buckets

Enamelled and zinc-galvanised buckets crop up in the most unlikely places: boot fairs, flea markets and junk shops, sheds, cellars and lofts. In general, buckets are only thrown away when they're no longer watertight. Perfect! Otherwise a hole-punch and a hammer will supply all the drainage your plants need.

chimney pots

From more-or-less plain pipes to those especially designed to embellish rooftops and others with windproof louvres, old chimneys pots act as combined plant pots and plinths. Architectural salvage yards usually have the best ones, but many can still be picked up for a song. Find a suitably sized plastic flowerpot that will slip into the top, grow upright plants in decorative chimneys so as not to obscure their

details, and save danglers for pots that are nothing to write home about.

crates

Not only are wooden crates beautifully proportioned for planting, they also stack securely. This means you can have a row of containers at different heights – and the supporting crates can be used for storing hand tools, bags of compost, seed trays and flowerpots.

food and drink containers

Look at catering-sized tubs and tin cans that once held mayonnaise, gherkins or tomatoes. Think about whole or halved beer, wine or whisky barrels. Imagine what you could cook up in old saucepans, colanders, kettles and teapots.

roof tiles

Ridge tiles can hold succulents just as they are. Semi-cylindrical Mediterranean tiles can be mounted against the flat variety to make great wall planters. It's a really nice touch to use the same tiles as those on the roof of your home. If someone down the road is having their house re-roofed, make them your new best friend.

sinks and troughs

Shallow stone or stoneware sinks show off alpines and succulents to perfection. To prevent water stagnating in them ensure that there's a gentle slope towards the plughole and use plenty of drainage crocks over it. Deep stone troughs provide a cool root run for larger, more dramatic, plants.

wheelbarrows

There's nothing sillier than those ridiculous flat-pack wooden wheelbarrows sold in garden centres, but there's nothing more satisfying than seeing the genuine article give sterling service long after retirement. The drill, as ever, is good drainage.

10 ideas

as you sow so shall you reap

Hurry, demand instant results, and you'll never get the best from your plants. Take time to ponder, take care to treat them well, and you'll be amply rewarded for your patience.

Plants – 'soft landscaping' in commercial terms – come at a fraction of the price of hard landscaping, yet they take all the glory if you get them right. Some plants are grown mainly for their foliage, others are chosen for their flowers. They can all be grown from seed, bought as youngsters, or installed as mature specimens. A thoughtful combination of all three approaches gives the best results.

Choose plants that you like and try not to be swayed by others. Pundits praise a plant one year then decry it the next, but the bottom line is if something really appeals to you, give it a whirl; if it doesn't, wait for something else that does. Don't be rushed, and do everything in your own good time.

And to make sure you have wonderful things in your garden during winter, too, allow me to share a tip: go browsing for plants regularly, buy them in their prime if you can, and you'll have something in bloom all year round.

structured planting

Plants literally bring gardens alive, but well-structured plantings bring them alive visually. To achieve success at this level you need to consider the shape and habit of each plant and to make sure you have variety and focus.

Some plants thrust vigorously upwards, others weep, some hug the ground. They can be dense and bushy, loose and billowing, large-leaved or small. Think about which look you like, what is already present in your garden and what is missing. Think about contrasts and combinations. Consider what might complement your hard landscaping, decorative features and furniture.

Paint a picture of your garden in your mind's eye: sketch out the foreground, the middle ground and the background. Scan across the scene from left to right to check there's always something of interest in your field of vision. Near or far, this side or that, you need distinctive shapes to focus on. Mentally overlay new planting elements on the existing scene. This sort of creative visualisation helps enormously in deciding precisely what you need.

topiary 82

Achieved by pruning, training and clipping trees or shrubs into figurative, geometric or abstract shapes, topiary not only effects a smooth transition from the buildings and hard landscaping into the more natural world, it also brings welcome definition to loose informal plantings.

Gardens of the past often had a parterre – a flowerbed with topiary borders – or a knot garden – a more elaborate conceit with small hedges laid out in criss-crossing patterns trimmed to look as though they are woven together. Both provide formal compartments for plants that look a little unruly when left to their own devices – herbs in particular are perfect ingredients.

getting into shape

Evergreen, dense and with very small leaves, boxwood (*Buxus sempervirens*) and yew (*Taxus baccata*) are the all-time classic subjects for topiary and are much-loved components of historic European and North American gardens. They require only two cuts a year – once in late spring then again in late summer – so maintenance is easy. The sooner in a plant's life you begin clipping, the better. Trimming back the growing tips promotes more and more side shoots, creating an ever tighter network of tiny branching stems. Work over young plants by eye, then as they mature use canes or wires as templates. For example, one bamboo stick is all you need to trim

a cone; four of them will give a pyramid; a hoop will form the perfect sphere. Animal shapes have more character trimmed freehand but you can make or buy open wirework armatures if you're worried about mistakes. Pause and stand back at regular intervals to monitor your progress.

think outside the box

• *Berberis* Barberry can be treated just like box but is much faster-growing. It has the benefit of yellow to orange flowers in spring.

• *Cotoneaster* Trim this early in summer once the white or pinkish flowers have died away. As with the barberry, this means you won't have any berries to speak of in autumn.

• *Eleagnus* Resistant to wind, salt and drought, this silvery-leaved or yellow-variegated shrub is ideal near the coast or in scorching sun.

• *Ilex* Holly is ideal either for large-scale 'lollipops' or for freeform 'cloud' formations on multiple stems.

• *Laurus nobilis* Bay is a handsome subject that needs pruning only once a year in late summer. Half leaves look raggedy after the trim and should be removed by hand.

• *Lonicera nitida* This fast-growing evergreen honeysuckle does well in shade but only stays compact if given several trims a year. 'Baggesen's Gold' has striking yellow leaves.

keep it evergreen

If you think of topiary as your anchorage, then larger-leaved evergreens are the mainsails that keep your garden up to speed and right on course throughout the year, whatever the weather.

Araucaria araucana

Native to Chile and Argentina, this strange conifer has spiralling scale-like leaves wrapped tightly round every branch. Although slow-growing it will ultimately reach a height of around 20m and a spread of 10m.

Arbutus unedo

This acid-lover ultimately attains a height and spread of 8m. Bay-like leaves are joined by small dangling white flowers in autumn that ripen over the course of a whole year into strawberry-sized leathery red fruits.

Eriobotrya japonica

This 8m Himalayan tree doesn't look evergreen at all. But it is. The loquat's dark green leaves are felted and silvery below up to 30cm in length. It requires a warm and sheltered site.

Eucalyptus

The gum tree is a sun-lover that can acclimatise to harsh winters over a few generations. Buy a specimen from as local a nursery as possible to be sure of success. Don't leave it to its own devices or it will grow enormous. Grow it as a multi-stemmed shrub instead by cutting it almost to the ground each spring.

Phormium tenax

The sword-like leaves come heavily striped in cream, yellow, pink or purple according to variety. Some stand erect while others are gently arched. Allow for a height and spread of around 2m.

Fatsia japonica

The deeply lobed leaves are up to 30cm across. If a mock castor-oil plant can survive its first few winters without too hard a frost it'll harden off nicely and you'll have a rounded shrub with a spread of up to 4m.

Magnolia grandiflora 'Exmouth'

The huge glossy leaves of this variety are tough as old boots. The creamy white late-summer flowers look like water lilies. It's a real beauty, but one that needs a lot of space as it can grow to a staggering 20m if left unpruned.

Mahonia

With its holly-like leaves, its leggy palm-like habit, and its intensely fragrant flower plumes in late winter, this 2m shrub would cause a riot if it were a new introduction.

Viburnum rhytidophyllum

A 5m shrub with large, rough, deeply veined leaves. Massed white flower heads in spring give way to glossy red fruit that ripen to black.

Yucca gloriosa

A proud, palm-like plant to 3m tall with rosettes of 50cm leaves sharp as daggers. *Y. flaccida* is more reliably hardy but it never grows much of a stem.

84
the march of the seasons

The hardest times of year to cater for are late autumn, winter, and early spring. Garden centres allow their stocks to dwindle, and many small nurseries close their doors altogether, so the idea of buying plants in season falls flat on its face. There is a solution though. Don't plough laboriously through gardening encyclopaedias, visit parks and gardens open to the public and note down *their* contents instead. Look out for especially late- or early flowering bulbs, for berried treasures that carry their fruit right through winter, for shrubs with scented blooms or catkins full of pollen.

autumn

• *Anemone* x *hybrida*
Japanese anemones have pink or white flowers on tall wiry stems.

• *Aster novae-angliae*
New England asters in white, pink, red or purple are stars of autumn borders.

• *Clematis* 'Bill Mackenzie'
Lemon-yellow blooms with petals thick as orange peel.

• *Echinacea purpurea*
Deep pink petals around a prominent orange-brown boss.

• *Rosa moyesii*
Summer flowers give way to long-lasting bottle-shaped hips in brightest scarlet.

winter

• *Adonis amurensis*
Buttercup yellow flowers followed by fernlike foliage.

• *Cyclamen coum*
The shuttlecock blooms and silver-patterned foliage thrive in dry shade under trees.

• *Erica carnea*
The winter heath tolerates a wide range of soils and flowers from early in winter to the beginning of spring.

• *Iris unguicularis*
The Algerian iris is so tough that the violet-purple flowers often poke right through snow.

• *Sarcococca*
Winter box is an evergreen with tiny white flowers of piercing fragrance.

spring

• *Camellia*
Often grown in pots because they require ericaceous compost, the waxy blooms of hybrid camellias are worth all the trouble.

• *Chaenomeles japonica*
The orange-red blossom precedes the leaves on this thorny shrub.

• *Crocus tommasinianus*
This precocious little bulb bursts into a bloom a full month before the ordinary spring crocus *C. vernus*.

• *Doronicum orientale*
The large yellow daisy-like flowers of leopard's bane can be single or double according to the variety.

• *Paeonia suffruticosa*
The Moutan peony has enormous blooms to 30cm in diameter.

for now and always

85

Once your evergreen bone structure is in position and you've come to terms with the fact that your garden will change with the seasons, you can finally think about colouring it in with flowers. Consider the relative heights of different flower stems; the size, shape and bulk of the blooms; how to combine their hues and tones.

annuals

Germinating in spring, flowering in summer, then setting seed in autumn, annuals like sunflowers, poppies, candytuft and nigella complete their short but sweet life cycle in a single year. They are a quick, cheap and cheerful way to fill your garden with a mass of colour.

biennials

Plants like foxgloves, hollyhocks and evening primroses put on leafy growth in their first season then burst into flower the next. Allow them to self-seed around your garden like exclamation marks. Pull out any that land in annoying places!

perennials

These have real staying power. Hellebores that bloom in winter, primroses that flower in spring, summertime delphiniums and autumn asters, they all go on year after year. They form larger and larger clumps that can be lifted and divided to make new plants for growing elsewhere or for swapping with friends. They're the slowest plants to get established and the most expensive to buy, but they give the best long-term return.

five favourite combinations

1 • Pink roses underplanted with forget-me-nots, lady's mantle and lavender – and with some seedlings of *Verbena bonariensis* slipped in for a brilliant purple haze dancing up above.

2 • Contrast the flat yellow flowerheads and fernlike foliage of achillea with rich blue irises and their swordlike leaves. Throw some towering verbascums into the mix and scatter white snapdragons all around.

3 • The scented yellow flowers of *Hemerocallis citrina* open in the evening and only last a day, but there's a never-ending supply in midsummer. With white lupins, evening primroses and *Nicotiana* 'Lime Green' they look especially fresh and bright.

4 • Plant any red-hot poker you fancy, add *Crocosmia* 'Lucifer', *Rudbeckia* 'Herbstsonne' and *Dahlia* 'Bishop of Llandaff' then reach for your sunglasses.

5 • Catmint, *Osteospermum* 'Pink Whirls', *Geranium* 'Johnson's Blue' and the mealy sage *Salvia farinacea* f. *alba* always look flouncy and pretty together.

86

the scented garden

Choosing plants for scent as well as looks doubles the appeal of any outdoor space. Some scents are so delicate or fleeting that you must go right up to a bloom to experience the magic. Others, powerful and captivating, proclaim from afar. Perfume encourages us to linger, to retrace our steps and track it to its source, to close our eyes and drink it in. The greater the variety, the headier the cocktail and the more fascinating your garden. For year-round appeal, select plants when they're in bloom and be led by your nose.

12 all-time greats for flower scent

1 • *Buddleja davidii* Lusciously redolent of honey.

2 • *Convallaria majalis* Piercingly sweet lily-of-the-valley loves damp shade.

3 • *Dianthus* 'Mrs Sinkins' The most enticing clove-scented aroma of all the pinks, carnations and sweet williams.

4 • *Erysimum cheiri* Wallflowers have a warm velvety fragrance that is rich, ripe and fully rounded.

5 • *Hamamelis mollis* Sharp, clean, astringent witch hazel.

6 • *Hyacinthus orientalis* Breathtaking hyacinths have conquered the world.

7 • *Lavandula angustifolia* Drenches the air with the true scent of lavender.

8 • *Lilium regale* For opulence and sensuality the regal lily has no rivals.

9 • *Nicotiana sylvestris* Especially fragrant as evening falls.

10 • *Philadelphus* 'Belle Etoile' The mock orange is less sickly yet more powerful than true orange.

11 • *Reseda odorata* The migonette is an inconspicuous annual with a lingering scent.

12 • *Rosa* 'Gertrude Jekyll' A powerful Old Rose fragrance.

aromatic foliage

Aromatic leaves make a long-term accompaniment to seasonal flowers. Some have animal undertones as sensual as musk, civet and ambergris. Use them in the background to add mystery and depth.

• *Buxus sempervirens* (Box) foxy
• *Ribes atrosanguineum* (Flowering currant) pungent
• *Ficus carica* (Fig) musky
• *Humulus lupulus* (Hops) bitter
• *Ruta graveolens* (Rue) acrid

Foliage plants can also be fresh, spicy and invigorating. Perfect for growing along pathways or for planting in pots beside seats and tables, they release essential oils each time you brush by. For a more intense hit, crush a leaf or two between your fingers. Instant aromatherapy!

• *Prostanthera rotundifolia* (Australian mint bush) blackcurrant cough linctus
• *Mentha* x *piperita* f. *citrata* (Eau de Cologne mint) the name says it all
• *Artemesia abrotanum* (Lad's love) bitter lemon
• *Aloysia triphylla* (Lemon verbena) fresh lemon zest
• *Pelargonium graveolens* (Scented geranium) rose and citrus scents

8–7

the herb garden

Herbs not only make a tasty health-giving contribution to our diet, they are also fun and beautiful to grow.

in the garden

The common culinary herbs come mostly from Mediterranean climates, so they grow best of all in warm, sheltered and sunny spots. Balm, basil, bay, bergamot, mint, parsley, pennyroyal and sorrel like rich, moist earth. Hyssop, marjoram, oregano, rosemary, sage, savory, tarragon, thyme, dill and fennel prefer dry, well-drained soil.

containers

Parsley and fennel have long tapering roots so never do well in containers. As for the others, give all of them the kind of compost they like and water them according to their needs. Special herb pots with large holes in their sides are an efficient way of growing a lot of herbs in a tiny

space; just remember to buy two –
one to fill with peat and rich
leaf-mould, the other with a gritty
soil-based mix.

window boxes

Two window boxes on your kitchen
sill where you can give them plenty
of attention can supply almost all
your needs. Skeins of moisture-
loving Indian mint (*Satureja
douglasii*) are a good choice for
trailing down the front, as are young
plants of prostrate rosemary.

hanging baskets

The bushier, drought-loving herbs
are the best candidates for hanging
baskets. Thyme and oregano work
well around the sides. Marjoram,
sage, savory and rosemary are better
up top.

colours

Look out for varieties with coloured
or variegated leaves:
• Purple sage (*Salvia officinalis*
    Purpurascens Group)
• Bronze fennel (*Foeniculum vulgare*
    'Purpureum')
• Golden oregano (*Origanum
    vulgare* 'Aureum')

• Variegated lemon balm (*Melissa
    officinalis* 'Aurea')
• Tricolour sage (*Salvia officinalis*
    'Tricolor')

flavours

Different varieties of the same
species can have radically
different flavours. Mint and thyme
in particular can be fruity or spicy:
• *Mentha suaveolens* green apples
• *Mentha suaveolens* 'Variegata'
    ripe pineapple
• *Mentha* x *gracilis*   ginger
• *Thymus* x *citriodrus*   lemon
• *Thymus herba-barona*   caraway

convenience

Whether they're in pots or in the
ground, it's a good idea to grow
your herbs close by the kitchen
door. Rosemary branches within
reach of a barbecue are great for
brushing oils or marinades onto
meat as it cooks.

harvesting

Whenever you need to harvest a
few whole sprigs of this or some
leaves of that, don't pick them at
random. Pinch out what you need
from the ends of the stems to

encourage branching further
down. This gives fuller, better-
looking and infinitely more
productive plants.

cooking

Herbs have a far finer flavour
fresh than dried but you need to
use them more generously than
their spice-rack counterparts.
Freshly gathered herbs have a
high moisture content; dried
ones lingering around in jars are
concentrated dust.

tisanes

Fresh herbal infusions
sweetened with honey or white
sugar are refreshing
alternatives to tea
and coffee. Pour
boiling hot
water over the
leaves and let
them steep for
several minutes
before straining the
brew into cups. Moroccan mint
(*Mentha spicata* 'Moroccan') is a
stimulant; the flowers of
Chamaemelum nobile make
soothing chamomile tea.

**10
ideas**

consuming passions 88

An edible garden can be just as decorative as a flower garden.

10 ideas

good enough to eat

Mix herbs, fruit and vegetables in amongst your blooms, call the whole thing a potager, and suddenly you're rather smart. Fruit trees look beautiful anywhere but forget about root vegetables where space is tight. You'll be surprised at how quickly you can get some edible results.

radishes

These can be on your table just a couple of weeks after sowing. The younger they're eaten, the more succulent they are – so unlike the produce in the shops.

swiss chard

Grow this at the front of your borders. Choose varieties with stems coloured yellow, orange, red or purple. The leaves can be used whole in salads when young. When mature – only a couple of months after sowing – the greenery can be cooked like spinach, the midribs can be eaten like asparagus.

cut and come again mixed salad

This is yours for the snipping. Buy a ready-made mixture of seeds or make your own. Rocket, endive, land cress, mache purslane and red amaranth are exciting additions to loose-leaved lettuces like 'Funly', 'Grand Rapids', 'Lolla Rossa' and 'Oak Leaf'.

stir-fry vegetables

Choose colourful, peppery, well-flavoured leaves like Chinese cabbage, kale 'Red Russian', leaf radish, mibuna, mizuna, mustard and pak choi. Grow some clumps of perennial spring onions for added bite.

cherry tomatoes

Because these are small they ripen really fast. Some varieties can even be grown tumbling charmingly out of hanging baskets and window boxes!

fruit trees

Don't dismiss top-fruit like apples, pears, cherries, figs, plums and apricots because they grow on trees. They can be grafted onto dwarfing rootstocks to restrict their size and trained into manageable shapes that even the smallest of gardens can accommodate:

• **cordon** – single stem grown at an angle and trained on posts and wires or along walls; especially suitable for apples and pears.

• **fan** – low central stem with radiating arms; encourages heavy cropping in stone fruits and in figs.

• **espalier** – central stem with paired horizontal arms branching out at the sides.

stepover – horizontally trained cordons that can be used as edging for beds.

grapevines

These are incredibly hardy but require a hot sunny wall for the fruit to ripen well in cool climates. Prune them hard in winter for a strong woody framework rather than a mass of winding twigs. Thin out the young grapes in each cluster with a sharp pair of scissors so there's plenty of space for the remainder to plump out into.

cane and bush fruits

Cane fruits like raspberries and blackberries, and bush fruits like currants, gooseberries and blueberries have a tendency to spread so really require a larger-than-average garden. That said, there's always room for the odd plant or two to supply you with luxurious garnishes for breakfast cereals and desserts.

strawberries

Huge crops can be grown in purpose-designed towers in really small gardens or on balconies. They also make excellent groundcover under rosebushes. For fruit you can't get your hands on in any other way, grow tiny fragrant *fraises des bois*.

3

part three

keeping it fresh

nature and nurture

Healthy soil is the key to healthy plants. Besides N, P and K – nitrogen for healthy greenery, phosphorous for roots and potassium for flowers and fruit – soil holds minuscule doses of hundreds of trace elements and minerals that are essential to growth. Oxygen, carbon and hydrogen from the air and from water are essential too. That's why plants not only need well-aerated free-draining soil that won't stagnate, but also soil that contains well-rotted organic matter that can soak up and hang on to moisture. It sounds complicated but Mother Nature knows what she's doing.

an exercise in fertility

Instead of chucking out kitchen peelings, tea leaves, coffee grounds and other raw vegetable waste, why not turn them into compost that you can dig into your soil? Compost bins come in all shapes and sizes. Plastic ones are cheap and readily available, but they're not the prettiest things in the world so camouflage them with potted plants or tuck them somewhere out of sight. More complex systems come with a supply of worms to hasten the composting process – these produce a really fine and crumbly compost, but they can be whiffy. Best of all are handsome wooden bins built to look like beehives. No need to hide these at all – they deserve pride of place in your garden.

watering

Watering is most effective either in the cool of the evening or early in the morning before there's any real heat from the sun.

Using a can might be time-consuming, but it's the most eco-conscious approach as you can single out the plants that most need your attention.

Hosepipes and sprinklers deliver an awful lot more in a fraction of the time but they're very wasteful and you're often left with dry spots under large-leaved plants. Water droplets left on foliage act as tiny magnifying glasses and can lead to scorching in bright sunshine.

Irrigation systems are expensive to install but they take all the hard work out of your hands: controls range from simple mechanical timing devices to computer-monitored soil- and atmospheric-moisture sensors. Trickle systems using drip nozzles can take water to individual pots and hanging baskets; heavily perforated 'leaky pipe' can be run through beds and borders.

Having got your water into the soil, you want to keep it there. This is where mulching comes in: a surface layer of compost, bark chips, cocoa husks or gravel allows water to penetrate downwards but keeps evaporation to a minimum. Organic mulches deliver a double whammy: they are gradually incorporated into the earth, thus improving its 'sponginess' and making it more moisture-retentive.

pruning for growth

91

It may seem paradoxical, but you need to cut woody plants back so they can become big and strong.

• It is rudimentary garden hygiene to remove dead, damaged and diseased wood

• Pruning out awkwardly crossing branches improves appearances. It also prevents bark from chafing and exposing plants to infection.

• Thinning out crowded stems let in sunshine and fresh air.

• Cutting a single growing tip back encourages several shoots to break out below. It's a case of short-term loss for long-term gain.

• By pruning back long stems on flowering shrubs like roses you create multiple sturdy stems and get lots more flowers.

• Keeping fruit trees within bounds focuses their energy into fruit.

good timing

Prune just as winter turns to spring, before dormant buds spurt into active growth. The new stems will bear the coming year's flowers and fruit.

Early spring bloomers like forsythia and contrariwise shrubs like philadelphus and hydrangea are exceptions to this rule – prune them immediately after flowering.

tools of the trade

92

As with many jobs, it pays to get the right tools.

secateurs and gloves

Ratchet-action secateurs enable you to cut through really thick stems with a series of gentle squeezes. Always protect your hands as you work. Leather gloves are easily the best.

trowels and handforks

A trowel is the best tool for making a small flowerpot-shaped planting hole in the ground, and for scooping compost into containers. A handfork is for loosening earth and lifting plants out.

spades and forks

A smallish fork is all right for most jobs. Small-bladed spades are easier to use and their loads of earth are lighter.

watering cans and hosepipes

Choose a well-balanced can with a generously curved handle and with as large a capacity as you can comfortably carry. Retractable hoses do almost all the work for you, so there's no excuse for not putting them away when not in use.

93 spring into action

A season of burgeoning life, spring should rekindle your interest in the garden.

Pruning is one of the first things to do. Instead of hacking at everything in sight, tackle one plant at a time; you're a brain surgeon not an axe murderer. The more considered your approach, the better the results.

Cut down ornamental seedheads of flowering plants and the dead leaves of grasses. They've given you something to look at over winter but get rid of them sooner rather than later or you'll find them hard to disentangle from new growth.

Give your lawn – if you have one – the first cut of the year. Set the blades high and off you go!

In anticipation of great planting days to come, stock up on compost, containers, seeds and stakes.

94 summer madness

A good garden has its own momentum at the height of the growing season, so there's an awful lot to keep you busy.

staking

Many garden plants have been bred so intensively for their flowers that the stems can hardly bear the weight any more. Using garden canes to tie up every top-heavy stem is the obvious (and rather ugly) solution, but there's another that's less trouble and gives more discreet results. All it requires is forethought. Push twiggy sticks (sometimes called 'pea sticks') around your herbaceous perennials and tall-growing annuals very early in the season. As the plants grow they hide these supports completely and will have a more natural, less straight-laced appearance.

dead-heading

By removing spent blooms you prevent seedheads from forming and since plants want to perpetuate their species, their response to this treatment is to produce more flowers.

filling the gaps

Slam annuals in wherever you see a space, sow salad seeds or put in young tomato plants from a garden centre. Better to grow something worthwhile than leave room for weeds to grow.

mowing

Sorry, but yes! And weekly.

outdoors indoors

It's a poor garden indeed that can't spare a bunch of flowers for your own home or a friend. To make them last as long as possible pick them early in the morning and cut their stems on the diagonal so there's the largest possible surface area for absorbing water. If any bleed white latex, singe the tips in a flame or scald them momentarily in boiling water.

a clean sweep 95

Autumn is the best season for taking stock of your garden.

tidy your containers

Pots in particular, unless planted with evergreen perennials, begin to look redundant. Don't let them become cemeteries for summer bedding; sort them out and get them into shape ready for your next big display.

Uproot all your annuals and put them on your compost heap if you have one. Don't think for a minute of re-using the old potting soil – there won't be any nutrients left. Scatter it over your flowerbeds or throw it away.

Next, groom the plants that remain. Cut away any brown or damaged leaves. Pot root-bound specimens up into larger containers, and where that's not practicable, top-dress them by scraping away a few centimetres of tired earth and pouring in some fresh.

treat your furniture

If you're the foolish owner of furniture that has to be put away each winter, now's the time to clutter up your shed or garage. Other outdoor tables and chairs might need a little maintenance. Treated wood, while the weather's still dry, benefits from being lightly sanded then re-oiled, re-varnished or re-painted. This gives it the best protection through the wet and cold months ahead when water can seep into cracks and frost can work joints loose.

dirty corners

As you move things around you'll notice tidemarks of dirt in out-of-the-way places and pockets of slime, leaves and soil in patio corners. Brush them away or hire a power-hose for the day and jet-blast everything in sight.

other jobs

• Lift and divide garden perennials
• Prune tall shrubs and long branches on trees that look susceptible to wind-damage
• Harvest any remaining fruit or vegetables

winter warmers 96

Unencumbered by any pressing need to lift a finger, winter is the time for armchair gardening.

Deep in contemplation you can flick through seed catalogues and nursery lists to track down interesting plants that you've read about or seen on your travels. Having watched your garden over the course of a year you'll be aware of spaces that need filling and areas that could be developed from scratch. Think about the shape of things to come.

If you've got a terrestrial garden rather than a rooftop or balcony garden, one job that is best done in winter is digging. Frost helps to break up clods of earth, so if you turn over the soil now in preparation for flowers or a lawn, Mother Nature will lend a helping hand.

Something else you can do is to get rid of clutter (see 97).

out with
the old

97

We have no qualms about composting or burning fallen leaves. It's all part of a natural cycle that makes way for the new. Apply that principle to everything in your garden.

For example, flowerpots given as presents by well-meaning friends won't always match your style. The worst offenders always shatter in frost, if you catch my drift. The crocks are good for drainage in containers that you do like.

Dealing with other people's rubbish is one thing, sorting our own is more traumatic. That's why so many of us hang on to broken tools, to plants that are ailing or moribund, to more seed trays and plastic pots than the most efficient nursery could ever fill. Not to mention wonky furniture, centuries-old tins of paint and other household detritus that finds its way into sheds, garages and the garden itself. It won't come in handy one day. It's an eyesore. It's holding you back. And it's taking up precious space. Just let it go.

storage

These stylish, original ideas may well set you off thinking of your own storage solutions.

all on show

Equipment can often be hidden in plain sight. Create a tableau of tools and watering cans on an outdoor wall all ready for use. Purpose-made hooks are easily bought but they may need repainting as garden-centre colours always veer towards the garish.

false friends

Get rid of all superfluous nonsense in your shed and hide what remains in a cupboard-like false wall flush against the back. Then you can open up the front of your shed completely and use it as a summerhouse.

a cunning plan

Hide hand tools and the odd bag of compost in a tall planter with a dish of shallow-rooted evergreens slipped cunningly into the top.

settle in

Buy a settle-like bench with a box base and a flip-up seat.

traps and tricks

Build a trapdoor into raised decking.

where there's a will
there's always
a way to
make
stuff
go
a
w
a
y
!

5 ideas

broaden your horizons

To give yourself a constant source of fresh ideas, try some or all of the following:

1 • Travel further afield for interesting and unusual plants, objects and materials. You get a day out to boot.

2 • Check out the mail-order catalogues of specialist nurseries. Bear in mind that some plants will only be despatched in late spring or early autumn when they're more or less dormant.

3 • Read gardening magazines and newspaper columns and scan the adverts for new garden products and services.

4 • Watch television gardening programmes and listen to those on the radio. Television is a great source of inspiration – and you get to see gardens that you could never visit in person. Local radio gardening slots are especially good sources of information that's directly relevant to your area.

5 • Join your national horticultural society. Flower shows, journals, lectures and specialist gardening advice are just some of the benefits.

quick-fix tips for easy entertaining

When someone special is coming round to our home, or when we're entertaining a large crowd, most of us feel the need to whirl around making sure everything is just right. It's the same with barbecues and summer garden parties. Our garden might be good enough for ourselves but we want to make it extra special for our guests. Here's how . . .

lawns

If you've got one, give it a trim a few days ahead. A brand new haircut looks desperate.

hard surfacing

Give gravel paths a good raking over. Hose down your patio. Spruce up your decking with a mild soapy scrub.

boundaries and structures

Fences, sheds and pergolas can be re-painted or re-stained, hedges can be trimmed, wall shrubs can be clipped to remove old leaves and dead flowers.

containers and flowerbeds

Tidy up what's already there then if it looks a little spartan, slap in a few pots of bright, cheap and colourful annuals that are already in full bloom.

finishing touches

Arrange your furniture in conversational groups. Light a few scented candles before your guests arrive. If the party might go on into the evening, put some instant lighting in position ready for use.

yourself

Let the garden speak for itself. Put all your effort into being a great host or hostess.

101

relax and
enjoy

index

acknowledgements

All photography by Marianne Majerus except page 61 from Garpa Garden and Park Furniture.

Garden design by: 2 (left) Joe Swift; 2 (centre) Nicole Albert with Gardens & Beyond; 2 (right) Kevin Wilson; 3 (right) Dan Pearson, The Merrill Lynch Garden/RHS Chelsea 2004; 7 Declan Buckley; 10 Beth Chatto Gardens; 11 Michèle Osbourne; 12 Robin Cameron Don; 13 (below) Diana Yakeley; 14 Declan Buckley; 15 Paul Thompson; 20 Gardens and Beyond; 21 Peter Aldington ; 22 Gardens & Beyond; 23 Miranda Holland Cooper; 24–5 Lucy Sommers; 29 Kathy Lynam; 30–31 Christopher Bradley-Hole; 32 Michèle Osbourne; 33 Lindsey Knight, Brinsbury College, RHS Chelsea 2000; 35 Peter Chan & Brenda Sacoor; 36 Pat Wallace; 37 Robin Cameron Don; 39 Paul Cooper for Marston & Langinger; 40 Michèle Osbourne; 43 Michèle Osbourne; 44 Joe Swift; 45 & 46 (inset) Bunny Guinness; 47 Jill Billington; 48 Susan Bennet & Earl Hyde; 50 (below left & right) Jaques Wirtz; 53 Marie Clarke; 54 Ruth Collier; 54–5 Hazel Murray, RHS Chelsea 2003; 57 Bourton House, Glos; 58 (above) Stephen Anderton; 60 Claire Mee Designs; 63 (above left) Declan Buckley; 63 (below left) Ward & Bernard; 64–5 Kevin Wilson; 65 (inset) Christopher Masson; 66–7 www.spidergarden.com; 68 Judy Wiseman; 69 Claire Mee; 72–3 Susanne Blair; 74–5 Ballymaloe Cookery School, Co Cork. Ireland; 76–78 Michèle Osbourne; 79 Gay Wilson; 82 Aquasphere by Alison Armour Wilson; 83 Michèle Osbourne; 84–5 Declan Buckley; 88–9 Gardens & Beyond; 90 Mount Ephraim Gardens, Kent; 91 Terracotta container by Mark Pedro de la Torre; 93 Adam Caplin; 94 Grafton Cottage, Staffs; 95 Christopher Masson; 96 Walsham-le-Willows; 97 Christopher Masson; 99 Elsing Hall, Norfolk; 104 Terence Conran, RHS Chelsea 99; 106 West Dean Gardens, Sussex; 109 Christopher Masson.